ON DECORATION

ON DECORATION

David Brett

The Lutterworth Press
Cambridge

The Lutterworth Press
P.O. Box 60
Cambridge
CB1 2NT

British Library Cataloguing-in-Publication Data.
A catalogue record for this book
is available from the British Library.
ISBN 0-7188-2801-1

First published by The Lutterworth Press, 1992.

Printed and bound in Great Britain by
Redwood Press Limited, Melksham, Wiltshire

—Contents—

—*Acknowledgements*—

This book is the outcome of curiosity and pleasure. Its weaknesses are all my own, but in writing it I have had in mind a number of individuals. Barbara Freeman was with me on numerous journeys and took several of the photographs, later she read the first manuscripts. I am one of the many who have gained from studying with Gillian Naylor. Peter Stead was a helpful friend. Amongst the institutions that assisted me were the University of Ulster, whose McCrea Foundation enabled me to spend time as a Visiting Scholar at the Universities of Columbia and Pennsylvania. Colin Lester of The Lutterworth Press helped me reduce a mountain of material into a manageable form. To all of these, my thanks.

Most photographs were taken by myself or Barbara Freeman; but I would like to acknowledge the permission to reproduce photographs given by The Ulster Museum (pp. 8, 9); The Board of Trustees of the Victoria and Albert Museum (pp. 11, 13, 23, 24, 25, 33, 35, 37, 45, 46, 53, 61, 75); Royal Borough of Kensington and Chelsea (Leighton House) p. 40; *The Irish News* (p. 60); Glasgow Museums and Art Galleries (pp. 66, 67); The Hunterian Art Gallery, University of Glasgow, Mackintosh Collection (pp. 68, 69); The Glasgow School of Art (p. 71); The Bundesdenkmalamt, Wien, Austria (p. 79); and lastly to Brian and Denise Ferran for opening their home to our camera (pp. 72, 73, 74).

Philadelphia Academy of Fine Arts

— Introduction —

This is a book about decoration and its uses and meanings. My aim is to give something of the same attention we pay to painting and to architecture to quite humble objects - wallpapers, textiles, pieces of furniture - and to interior design. It proposes a way of interpreting its topic which is, broadly speaking, ideological; that is to say it is concerned with the more or less unspoken assumptions and concepts that govern our thinking about modernity, social position, history and the future course of society. I write 'broadly speaking' because no single or specific hypothesis is developed in the pages that follow; this book is not a thesis.

It does, however, develop an intellectual narrative through its investigation of what I call the 'discourse of decoration'. I mean by this the complicated and developing interaction of ideas, professional practice, clienteles and marketing as it evolved through the nineteenth century toward the present day. This discourse, which purports to be about taste and uses concepts such as the 'beautiful', the 'fitting', the 'suitable', and the 'aesthetic' as opposed to the 'vulgar', is (I conclude) essentially addressed to the definition of modernity. It asks such questions as 'what, in this novel industrial society, is our relation to the past?', or 'what forms of decoration can best express contemporary experience?' These are some of the typical questions which continually re-occur in that process of transformation whereby a predominantly rural society becomes urban and industrial. Thus, though the examples I discuss are from particular times and places, the overall problematic is virtually global in its implications.

The discourse of decoration has two origins; both in the early nineteenth century. The first lies in the realm of architecture. For the nineteenth century, systems of ornament were what primarily determined the style of a building; questions about style were almost always questions about decoration rather than construction or the arrangement of rooms and spaces. Thus, there arose an extensive debate as to the appropriate decorative system and how it should be made and finished. The second origin lies in the development of a new profession, that of 'industrial artist', 'ornamentist' or 'designer'. Preparation for machine production required a new approach to drawing and to mould- and model-making, which in turn required methods of training, which in turn demanded a discussion about first principles. The huge expansion of the market for domestic goods of every kind, and the way that market was divided up for internal consumption and for export, stimulated a critical discussion about the kinds and categories of decoration.

This discussion, as the century progressed, was conducted through scholarly writings, articles and lectures as much as through actual designs, and took on its own logical impetus. Ornament and pattern came to be a ground upon which much larger, general issues could be debated; the style of your living rooms might come to be the object of intense, even moralistic scrutiny. The styles and patterns one chose, the methods of manufacture, the teaching of design, the practice of drawing and the taxonomy of styles all became matters of significant public interest and spread out from the professional world of designers into the lecture halls, journals, and newspapers of the day; into a rapidly growing literature, and into the novels of Dickens, the pages of *Punch* and the operettas of Gilbert and Sullivan.

The tendency was to treat questions of decoration with ever greater seriousness and to draw distinctions between decoration in its own right and, on the one hand, architecture and on the other, the pictorial arts. But the overall logical form also ensured, I shall argue, the collapse and demise of any coherent decorative style; thus leading to the rejection of ornament by the most self-consciously modern architects and designers, and to the dissolution of all traditional decoration.

The conclusion that finally emerges from this little study is that the discourse of decoration represents a fever chart; the patient in this case being late European culture and the fever being its transformation into a form of universal civilisation, in the course of which its identity and integrity is altered beyond recognition.

The book is in two parts. The first is by way of a photographic essay, in which the intellectual narrative is taken forward and exemplified by illustrations and extended captions. The argument is necessarily terse, and the intention is to present the reader with a field for exploration and an outline map to find a certain way through it. The field is that of ornamental and decorative art since the 1820s; the map is a logical structure whereby we can begin to interpret it. It may be useful to add here that I do not make any substantial distinction between the terms 'ornament' and 'decoration', but treat the latter as a more general term and the former as being mainly three-dimensional.

In choosing illustrations I have deliberately confined myself to examples within my own life-experience; to buildings I have visited, objects I have handled and patterns I have stood beside or walked upon. Though some will be well known, I have tried to avoid those iconic examples which are repeated and re-examined throughout the literature of the subject. Most of these examples are nineteenth century, for reasons which will become apparent.

Nearly all my examples are British, though there was a similar and interlocking conversation throughout Europe and America. What makes the British discourse most interesting is that it was the most intensive and extensive, and that very largely it performed the same intellectual function as the debates on painting did in France: that is to say it was the arena within which a modern sensibility was fashioned. When I step outside Britain, it is because the discourse (which had its inception here) could only be completed elsewhere.

The second section consists of an essay in which I enlarge upon and enrich the themes I have merely proposed in the narrative. These themes are all concerned with aspects of modernisation.

Modernisation - in which industrial production and a science-based technology are allied to the growth of mass education and bureaucracy - requires the destruction of age-old habits of thought and behaviour. Thereafter 'traditional' culture becomes a very problematic area whose continued existence has to be defended, asserted, and in certain cases even invented. The study of decoration reveals this process very clearly, and demonstrates some of the political and social tensions that ensue. The history of the decorative arts in the past one hundred and fifty years can be analysed in terms of contrasting ideological positions whose roots are in the struggle for mastery within sections of the dominant class. These roots are also deeply embedded in the intellectual foundations of modernisation and in particular the disruption of culture and qualitative thought by scientific positivism which, by undermining the basis of metaphor, renders traditional symbolism invalid and any decoration based upon it, meaningless. Thus, the study of decoration becomes part of the study of the many ways in which modern society searches for its meanings.

This search for meaning has both normative and critical dimensions; the one looks toward the world of industry, science, economic development and a global culture; and the other, critically, toward history, myth, craft production and national or local loyalties. These might easily be described in terms of 'modernist' and 'anti-modernist' tendencies; but a major theme developed in these pages is that both tendencies are constantly present in an authentically modern experience and that both were understood at the times in question as possible or alternative forms of modernity. It follows from this that the idea of a putative 'post-modernism' finds no logical support here.

* * * *

I have also made some assumptions. The most important of these is that the reader has an outline knowledge of the main movements in art and architecture since the first decades of the nineteenth century; that he or she has some understanding of the main philosophical disputes of the time and is cognisant of positivism, utilitarianism, the Darwinian controversy and the continual clash between different aspects of materialism and idealism. These intellectual matters underpin the entire discourse.

In more general terms, the decorative arts of the last century and a half have been far more often described than interpreted. Terms such as 'historicist', 'eclectic', 'conventional' and 'naturalistic' only take on analytic usefulness when they are part of a larger structure. That larger structure is the discourse as a whole and its location within ideology and the social realm. For this reason I am deliberately avoiding the categories of an earlier design history, such as 'The Aesthetic Movement' or 'Art Nouveau', not because they are not useful in other contexts, but because they are descriptive and taxonomic rather than interpretative.

A good deal of the larger structure is now hard to recover in detail. It is easy to describe the demand for different styles in terms of a demand for clear signs of status, but quite another matter to distinguish between the differing demands and the differing social formations and markets. Decoration, especially cheaper work, is nearly always ephemeral; so too are most manufacturers and their records. Frequently it is only the very best work that survives - which may be neither typical nor, from many perspectives, the most interesting. There is, however, an extensive literature in English on decoration and its theory, and it is the existence of this 'corpus' that makes the study of the discourse possible. It is a body of argument that deserves to be better known, for reasons I have indicated already and will explore further. To repeat; this book should be thought of as an attempt at an intellectual narrative, not a social or economic history.

At root is a larger assumption; that decoration is important. This was taken for granted in earlier times but is not so easy to sustain today. That this should be so is an outcome of the discourse we are to study. As the nineteenth century progressed, normative theory continuously raised the status of decoration to that of an avant-garde fine art; the arguments used were increasingly like those advanced in favour of non-representational painting. This can be seen as a transcendental justification for the role of design and the designer in an industrial culture. The critical tendency, with its emphasis upon 'tradition', craft and history was manoeuvered into a reactionary position and its products steadily downgraded into the visual equivalent of populism. The likelihood was always that the first would extinguish itself in the abandonment of ornament altogether, and that the second would expire in self-parody and kitsch. Such a moment would mark the end of the discourse, or its complete transformation.

This indeed is what happened in the second decade of the twentieth century, when there was a powerful and well-considered attempt to do without architectural ornament altogether, and to dismiss the decorative arts as irrelevant to modern life. This attempt, usually identified with 'International Style' architecture and geometric abstraction in painting was, I argue, as much an outcome of the discourse as it was of developments within painting or architecture themselves.

The desire for decoration, however, appears to be a cultural constant and is, historically, one of the defining characteristics of specific cultures. It is quite probable that the desire is rooted *au fond* in biological inheritance through the characteristics of our perceptual system. In either case, the attempt to do without decoration needs to be considered very carefully. And looked at more searchingly, architectural ornament may be said to have been transformed, deviously, into new principles of composition. Hence also the many attempts that have been made to create new and consistent decorative styles by recourse to the arts of painting and sculpture; attempts that have often been striking but have not endured.

Whatever may be the case - and I will attempt to define the problem - the collapse of the discourse went hand in hand with the utter disruption of any decorative continuity.

This is a point of argument that I wish to stress. Recent years have seen a number of attempts to assemble (yet again) a neo-conservative cultural programme of 'reform'. But as Jurgen Habermas has neatly observed, this programme 'shifts onto cultural modernism the uncomfortable burdens of a more or less successful capitalist modernization of the economy and society'.[1] Attempts to reassert 'traditional' continuity under such conditions lead to pastiche, especially in the domain of decoration. It may now be best to assume that there are no traditional values or practices that are not the after-images of perpetual innovation.

Yet the disruption of decoration has left a void, especially in architecture; and this void is seen, felt and obscurely resented. It has lead to an otherwise absurd over-valuation of antiques and older buildings and to a sense that modern design is inadequate or in some sense 'inhuman'. For something more than fifty years it has proved very difficult to produce an architectural ornament which is both convincing and consistent; successful attempts (and there have been some) have left few or weak progeny. On a smaller scale, as in textiles, surface pattern, ceramics and glassware, decorative work having any claim to quality has come increasingly to be informed by 'languages' emanating from the fine arts or from a fetishisation of technology. The most characteristic strategy today is to construct fleetingly consistent styles by means of an ingenious and imaginative assembly of objects and patterns derived from very diverse sources.

Thus the narrative, coming toward present times, begins to investigate what sort of decoration is meaningful without a consistent discourse. Indeed, a subsidiary aim of this book is to describe the story of decoration in such a way as to shed light on the present state of affairs, in terms which might make sense to today's decorative artists, designers and craftspeople.

In a short book one cannot do everything.

I have made no attempt at a serious sociology of decoration. As already suggested, this is a very large and obscure topic, and such treatment would require a very different kind of book.

Nor have I sought to link the discourse of decoration to developing concepts of femininity, except in the most cursory way. This is certainly a considerable gap in the picture. In all the periods under discussion here, most writing on decoration, and most marketing, was directed at women as the principal clients, purchasers and, to some degree, creators of decorative styles; and this is still the case. This aspect of the subject represents both an affirmation of a huge area of human action which women could claim for their own, and (notoriously) a limitation on women's experience - a special kind of unimportance. I am not, of course, here concerned with women as designers, but with design as a means whereby gender is defined and objectified. To have attempted that task would, once again, require a different kind of book to this. In addition, before such a question could be tackled with the depth and dispassion it requires, much more work would need to be done; and there are good reasons for thinking that this should be initiated on feminist premises.

This book is part of a growing literature on the subject of decoration, published and unpublished. At all points I am indebted to this, but I have kept footnotes down to the barest references for the sake of brevity. The bibliography at the end is arranged under headings that directly relate to stages in the argument, and is wide-ranging but idiosyncratic.

In the course of the following pages I attempt to cover a great deal of ground at high speed; the argument will sometimes be very compressed. But I hope that I have written nothing obscurely.

Note:

1. Habermas, J. 'Modernity - an incomplete project' reprinted in *PostModern Culture* ed. H. Foster; Pluto Press, London (1985) p.7.

— *Samples* —

Sample 1

There are good reasons to begin with printed cottons. They have some claim to be the first truly industrial mass-produced goods; the designs that they carry were produced by a new and mainly anonymous profession of 'ornamentist' or 'industrial artist'; and they were part of something we would now recognise as a consumer society comprised mainly of women as buyers and users (and to a large extent, producers). In that early consumerism we see all those features we recognise today - incessant invention and combination, with assertions, absorptions, reversals and counter-reversals of taste, all enmeshed with problems of investment, new technology and the creation of new markets. All the issues with which we have to deal in this book are raised in some form by a study of these textiles. Printed cottons were also the goods that carried, to the far ends of the earth, conventions of pattern that were often wholly divorced from the symbolic form-languages of the recipient cultures; they formed, thereby, an avant-garde of cultural hegemony, the first wave of global uniformity.

Minute floral patterns of this sort were the staple product of the cheaper end of the trade. The mechanisation of printing and the subsequent increase in the export of cottons from Britain led to the decay of 'traditional' pattern-making all over the world. These patterns are now perceived, in their turn, as 'traditional' and are frequently revived in a context of rural associations (see, for example, the Laura Ashley catalogue for 1986).

Both examples a) and b) come from the same well-made and probably expensive dressing gown, so at that moment we may assume that small repeats of this sort were in fashion. There is plenty of evidence

a) machine-printed cotton, c.1830. (Coll. Ulster Museum).

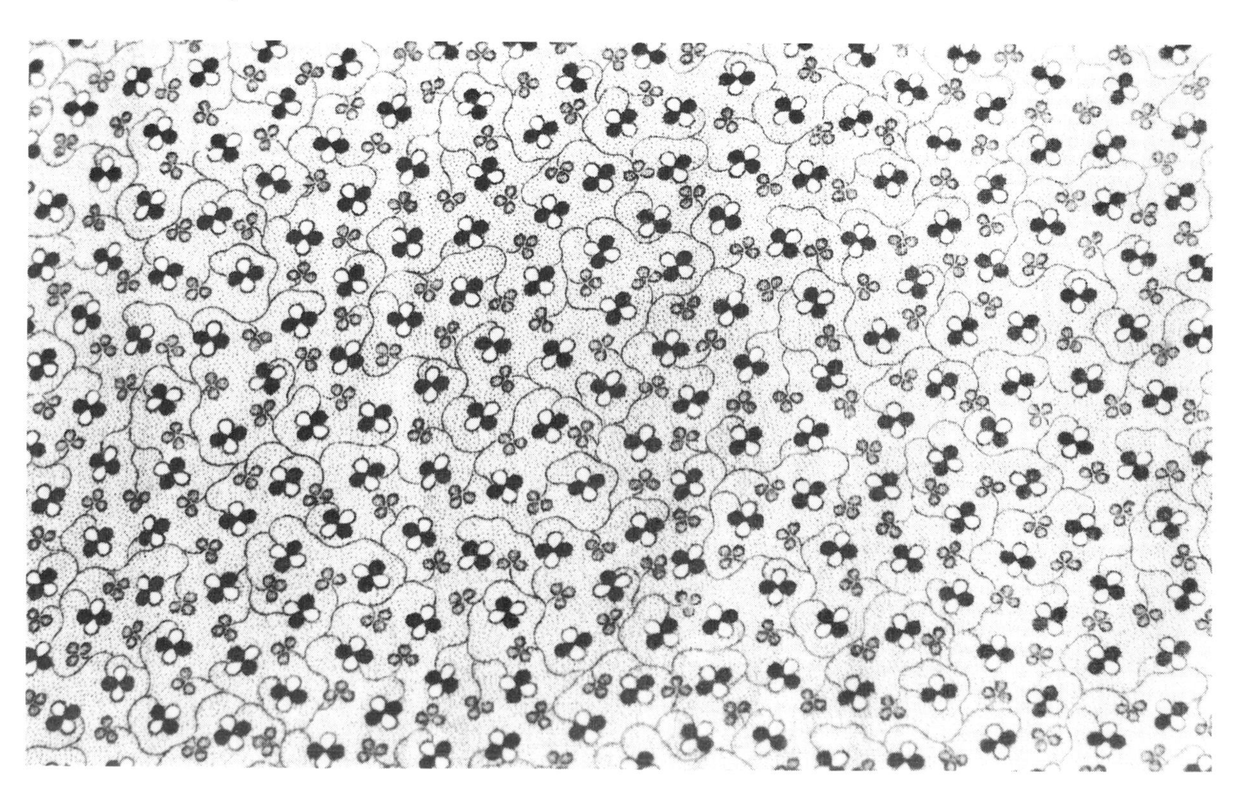

b) Another example, c.1830. (Coll. Ulster Museum).

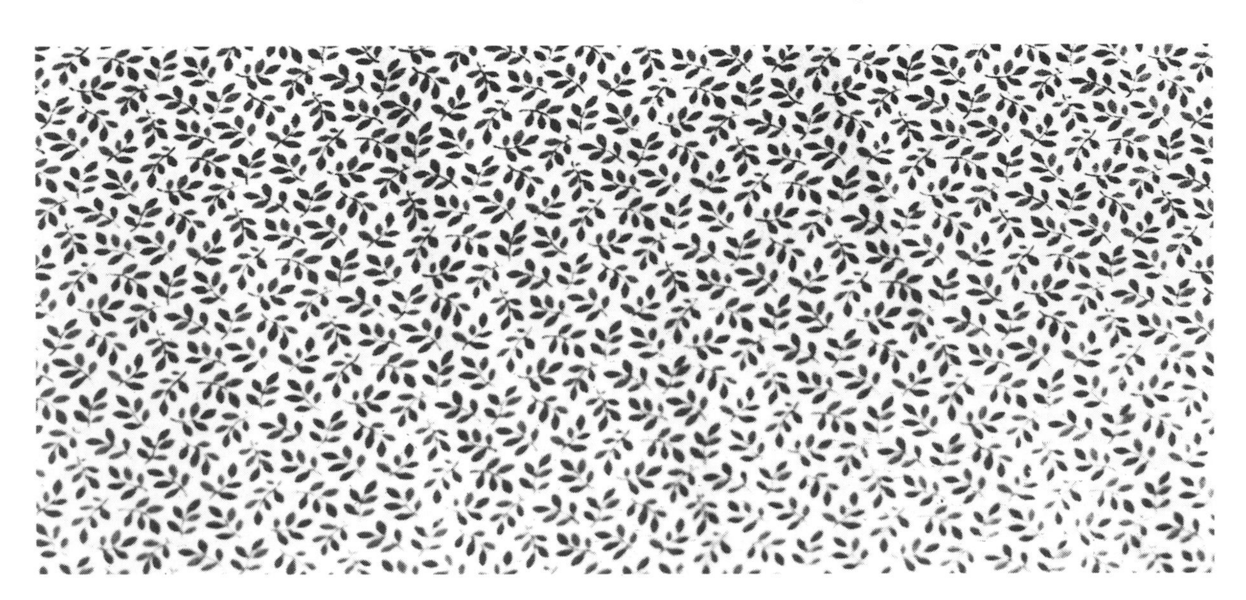

for a preference for simple repeat patterns, and one writer has seen this as typical of a stage in civilisation.

'Despite the many factors at work bringing design into being, the new machine-produced patterns can be seen, anthropologically, as the sign language of a people changing from a predominantly rural to an increasingly urban culture....the combination of the cylindrical never-ending surface, with the small mill and die, tended to produce overall patterns, minute florals, geometrics, and optical effects. The pervasiveness of the small repeat, in texture and motif, is so widespread that textile students today, when asked to produce a dress print, often instinctively produce designs of this sort.' David Greysmith (1980).

The example below is from a beautifully cut day dress with gigot sleaves. Thin red stripes on a plain white cotton ground give an overall pink bloom as fresh now as when it was first printed. A good example of up-market romantic simplicity.

c) Printed cotton, probably 1828. (Coll. Ulster Museum).

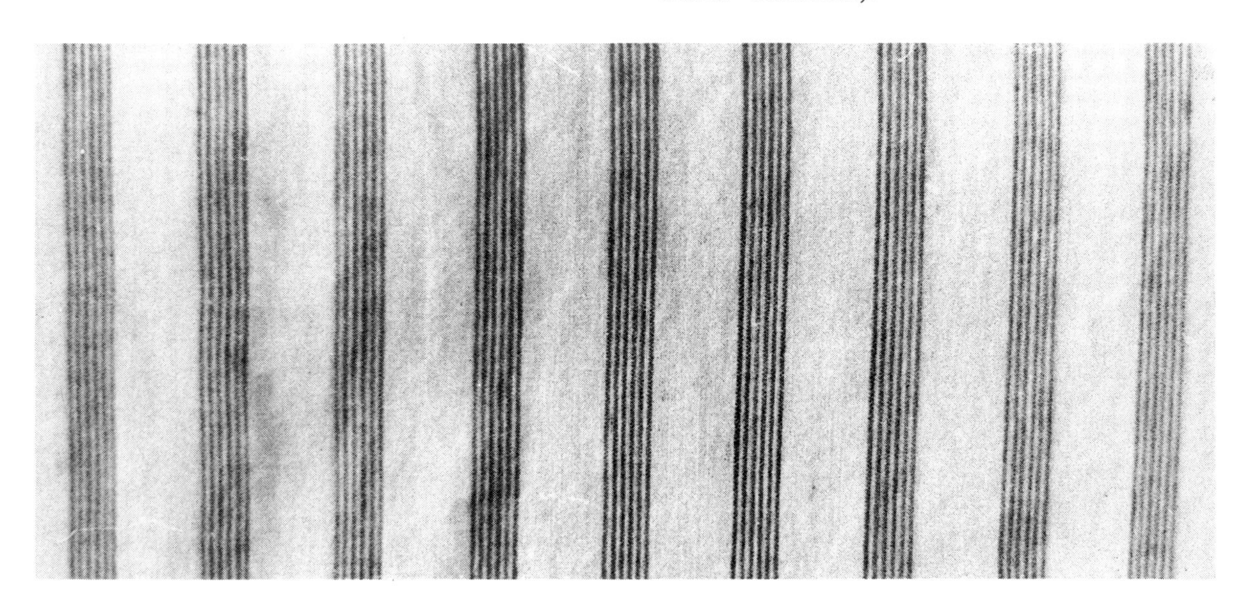

But how long did it take for the new technology to be capable of large expansive patterning? And who bought what designs? And for whom? And how long did it take for a design that had proved successful on top quality fabric to appear in a cheaper version on poor cloth? Similar patterns appear on wallpapers of the period: were the same engraved rollers used on both cotton and paper? To make matters more complicated, simple patterns were often seen as more suitable for servants (who had their clothes bought for them). Ginghams, simple florals and dots were produced in immense quantities, and as late as 1851, such designs were being published in *The Journal of Design and Manufactures* for a specifically working-class market. But gaudy and elaborate prints could quickly be produced just as cheaply. In a reaction of gentility, did the middle classes readopt the simplest possible patterning on the very best cloth; or even opt for plain white linen? There is evidence for this. And what about the practice of handing clothes down through the social scale, from mistress to maid and from maid to the used clothes market? Add to this the shorter lifespan of cheaper clothing, the disappearance of evidence, and we can see how difficult it is to get a clear picture of this rapidly developing area of decorative design.

Agnes Heller has described the growth of what she terms 'particularism', in which, in the flux of modernity, individuals construct a meaningful reality for themselves by identification with social norms. The particularist individual 'obtains (her) justification from direct identification with the system of customs' (Heller, 1979, p.155; and 1984, ch.2). Printed cotton dress fabrics provided one of the principal means of social differentiation and 'particular' choice that were available to women in the early nineteenth century; the means by which multiple and continually changing 'norms' could be identified. The rapidity and variety of patterning that we see in these printed cottons are part of the speeding up of fashion which is in turn an essential feature of a world in continual, capital-driven change.

Sample 2

An 'identification with the system of customs' is part of one's allocation into social groups and classes, more or less willingly. But whoever determines the norms is setting cultural boundaries. Choice of pattern - and wide choice was now available for the first time in history - signified social position and cultural status. (See Bourdieu, 1984, pp.56-57).

The more or less abstract and geometrical designs typical of the earliest machine-printed cottons were regarded as being in good taste by those who wrote about such matters. But there were also pictorial designs, in which flowers, vegetation, landscapes and sometimes architectural scenes were disposed at regular repeats over the surface, with the effect of perspective depth. These prints were frequently in imitation of more expensive hand-printed chintz patterns of earlier years. These designs catered to a taste for the picturesque and the two tendencies were seen as antithetical.

"Suppose you were going to carpet a room. Would you use a carpet having a representation of flowers upon it? . . ."

"If you please, sir, I am very fond of flowers" returned the girl. . . "They would be pictures of what was very pretty and pleasant, and I would fancy. . . ."

"Ay, ay, ay! but you mustn't fancy. . . you are not to have, in any object or use of ornament, what would be a contradiction in fact. You don't walk upon flowers in fact; you cannot be allowed to walk upon flowers in carpets. . .you never meet with quadrupeds going up and down walls; you must not have quadrupeds represented upon walls. You must see," said the gentleman, "for all these purposes, combinations and modifications (in primary colours) of mathematical figures which are susceptible of proof and demonstration. This is the new discovery. This is fact. This is taste." Charles Dickens, *Hard Times*, (1854).

a) Wallpaper, c.1840. Green roses and leaves on a brown ground. (Coll. Victoria & Albert Museum).

These are the two poles, established in the 1850s, around which tastes and the practice of design come together like iron filings round the two ends of a magnet.

Dickens' lampoon is, in fact, very accurate. He had been reading the *Journal of Design and Manufactures* and the writings of William Dyce, for whom the purpose of drawing was to form 'abstractions . . . of the operating and governing laws (of Nature) . . . which, by the very fact that they are abstractions, assume, in relation to the whole progress of art, the character of principles or facts, that tend by accumulation to bring it to perfection.' By these means, decorative design was to become 'a kind of practical science'. This is the extension of positivism from science into decoration.

But the demand for the pictorial did not disappear; twenty years later, Charles Eastlake was making the same complaint: 'if people will prefer a bouquet of flowers or a group of spaniels worked upon their hearthrug to the conventional patterns which are adopted by the Indian and Turkish weavers, it is difficult to convince them of their error.' (Eastlake, 1872 ed., p.116). He prints a number of simple abstract patterns constructed 'according to the true principles of design'.

b) Illustration from *Hints on Household Taste* by Charles Eastlake (3rd ed, 1872, p.12).

Later, I shall describe this little scene as a clash between the modernisers, and those who are being modernised. It shows a wedge being driven home, hard, to make a distinction between advanced and popular taste.

Sample 3

a) Wallpaper by A.W. Pugin; from the Palace of Westminster, 1845. (Coll. Victoria & Albert Museum).

And there was a third tendency, which was toward what I shall call emblematic decoration. This resembled the first in that it was largely abstract or 'conventional' in its drawing, but the motif had a distinct significance, as it would in heraldry and other well-recognised systems. There is no difficulty in reading the meaning of these patterns provided we have prior knowledge of the given system of signs, and their symbolic connotations. In such designs, the motif stands out from the ground, as an obvious pattern element, but the overall effect is to affirm the surface, rather than dissolve it into pictorial space.

This particular example is one of a set of powerful wallpapers printed for the newly rebuilt Palace of Westminster in 1845. With

b) Detail of carved ornament from Palace of Westminster. (Photo; the author).

their emblematic motifs and bold primary colours (bright blue, green and red upon white) these majestic patterns clearly represent the power of the state. Today, they can be seen most easily in the televised reports of the parliamentary committees.

Related to the many designs that Pugin produced for the interiors of churches, these wallpapers and the accompanying tile patterns for the Palace of Westminster are based upon carefully studied Medieval and Tudor precedents. Pugin and his followers carried this antiquarian approach to the practice of decoration from simple surface pattern right through onto the details of architecture, so that the entire surface of the building, within and without, could be 'read' for a distinct emblematic meaning.

Each of these three approaches to surface pattern develops its own theory of meaning, which unfolds in the succeeding decades. Each is distinguished by a different 'figure-ground' relationship, regardless of the ostensible motif, and these several relationships underlie the different associations of meaning that each had at the time, and still to some extent preserves. The struggle between them forms a major theme in the discourse.

Sample 4

'Although ornament is most properly only an accessory to architecture, and should never be allowed to usurp the place of structural features, or to overload or disguise them, it is in all cases the very soul of an architectural monument.' Owen Jones, *The Grammar of Ornament*, (1856).

a) Facade of the Palace of Westminster by A.W. Pugin, 1845. (Photo; the author).

Ornament was seen to carry the meaning of the building, by way of its historical associations or sign-language, yet it frequently had a merely arbitrary relation to the plan. The Palace of Westminster has a plan (by Barry) which has neo-classical symmetry, but the elevation and above all its ornament, surfaces, colours and textures are neo-Gothic. Had Owen Jones received the contract for the decoration instead of Augustus Pugin, we might well have had 'Moorish' Houses of Parliament - and this nearly happened.

Later, as part of the general rehousing of government during this period, Gilbert Scott designed a neo-Gothic Foreign Office to go with Pugin's Parliament, but was then asked to reclad it in 'Renaissance' dress. He found this request irksome but not essentially unreasonable. Pugin's proposal was accepted by the parliamentary committee on the grounds that the 'Gothic' was somehow more English than any other style, regardless of the fact that at the same time German and French architects and patrons were making exactly the same nationalistic claims. This nation-state imagery is present in the exterior details of the architecture as much as in the wall-hangings and murals within, and is 'read' from direct signs such as heraldry as well as the arrays of sculptured figures and the associations of ornamental mouldings.

Pugin brought to the task an approach to ornament that was rooted in an almost archaeological knowledge of the subject. He worked like a scientific historian, and had very definite ideas as to what was appropriate. He collected together the best examples from the real Gothic or Tudor past, and insisted that his workmen studied and copied them. This was one answer to the question - what is the style for industrial Britain? At first, a fanatical neo-Gothicism might seem an unlikely answer. When, however, we spend some time looking closely at these facades, it is easy to get the sense of a machine-like repetition and thoroughness that is nothing like the impression we get from a medieval cathedral, where we admire the variability and 'craft' quality of the detail. Pugin has treated these facades in the same spirit as he designed his wallpapers; as a continuously repeating system. Moreover, the enterprise required a reasonable level of industrial organisation to complete, and helped to promote the 'art industries' of Britain with great consequences for the future. Barry and Pugin's Palace of Westminster was the topmost project in a huge building programme undertaken by the state and by private and civic patrons during the third and fourth decades of the century; a vast corporate effort to house the first industrial nation. The tilemakers, metalworkers, plasterers, carvers, paperstainers and carpetweavers of Britain, confronted with more work than they had ever undertaken before, increasingly sought industrial methods of production and a wider range of retail outlets for their work.

Sample 5

a) St Vincent Street Presbyterian Church, part of the south elevation.(Photo; the author).

The Gothic may have been the most ubiquitous 'revival' of the nineteenth century, but it was by no means the only one. Every historical style was attempted, and some invented, in an attempt to produce an approach to building and decoration appropriate to time and place.

Scottish neo-classicism produced several fine architects but none more remarkable than Alexander 'Greek' Thomson. In the churches and villas that he built in and around Glasgow, he took the principles of classical building - post-and-lintel construction - in directions not dreamed of before; he was both antiquarian and proto-modern. This attitude passes over into his decoration, to which he devoted the most intense attention. What we find in the St Vincent Street Presbyterian Church, completed in 1859, is an extraordinary amalgam of classical, Egyptian, Hindu and other motifs mixed with geometrical and botanical elements and all brought into unity with the architecture by a sense of consistent scale and attention to detail. He also built many fine villas and terraced houses in a similar manner, which included specially matching furniture.

This encyclopaedic approach owes a good deal to the doctrines of the Department of Science and Art, as promoted through Owen Jones' compendium *The Grammar of Ornament* (1856). (See samples 7 and 12). Jones argued that a new style of architecture might be reached through a study of decoration rather than construction, and that the discovery of a new 'termination of the means of support' would be one step on the way.

The termination of this iron pillar (painted bright red, pink, green and gold) is one such attempt - a Scotto-Babylonish capital. The frieze above, in which the motifs and the ground balance harmoniously, and in which the stencilled character of the application is made clearly evident, is typical of the 'South Kensington school'. This manner passes over to the United States, and to the studio of Frank Furness (see sample 9).

Thomson used as his interior contractor a fellow Glaswegian, Daniel Cottier. Cottier in time became an important figure in the Aesthetic Movement of the 1880s, and ran an international business in fine and decorative arts. Through his agency, English aestheticism was serviced by Scottish designers and craftspeople.

b) Detail of the interior of St Vincent Street Presbyterian Church, Glasgow, designed by Alexander Thomson in 1859.(Photo; the author).

Sample 6

Glasgow is full of fine nineteenth-century buildings and few structures are more striking than Templeton's Carpet Factory on Glasgow Green. J.S. Templeton was a leading manufacturer of carpets. Amongst the designers who worked with him were Walter Crane and Charles Voysey. When he obtained this site, beside a public space, the city council insisted that the building should be of the highest quality. Templeton employed William Leiper, who had hitherto built neo-Gothic churches and a number of country mansions on the grandest scale, to produce this Veneto-Moorish fantasy-factory.

Several trains of argument come into collision across this facade: there is an overall 'Venetian Gothic' manner, inspired by Ruskin; there is the debate about colour and surface; there is 'Moorish' flat pattern; and there is the effect produced by mixing materials usually kept apart (plain brick,

a) Facade of Templeton's Carpet Factory, Glasgow. Designed by William Leiper in 1888. (Photo; Barbara Freeman).

b) Detail of facade of Templeton's Carpet Factory. (Photo; Barbara Freeman).

glazed bricks of several colours and tone, mosaic, carved red sandstone, carved Givnock sandstone, painted iron and terracotta). This is surely one of the most remarkable achievements of nineteenth-century commercial building.

Leiper's domestic buildings were all sumptuous and expensive, and included stained glass by leading Glaswegian painters and ceramic work by William de Morgan. He, too, employed Daniel Cottier. He was also an early example of an architect who designed the interior of ships. His designs for the yacht *Livadia* (1880), commissioned by the Tsar of Russia, were in a mixture of 'Louis XVI', 'Crimean Tartar' and 'the simplest kind of modern English' styles. This sounds a bizarre mixture, but Leiper might well have made sense of it. The intensity and quality of decoration and architectural ornament in the Glasgow area was by no means solely connected with buildings. The single largest source of demand was for the shipfitting trades, which employed skilled craftspeople and designers in enormous numbers. The speed and commercial rapacity of the Clydeside ship-builders was such that almost no records of this fascinating field remain. Huge, elaborately fitted-out ships were built of which no descriptions have survived. Thus, the study of decoration must always return to its architectural examples since they alone have a long life.

Sample 7

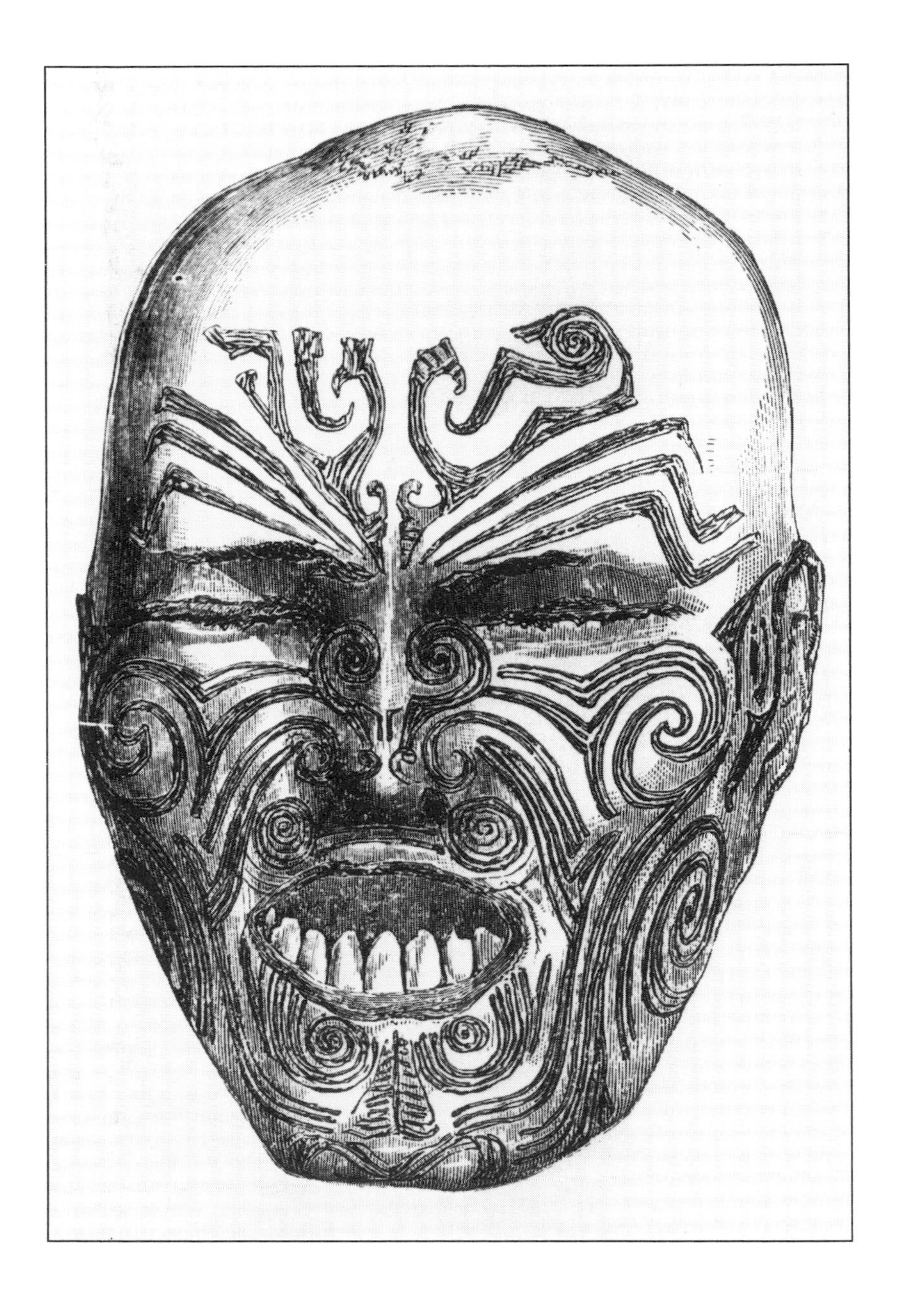

a) Maori head; from the introduction to *The Grammar of Ornament*, line block.

The extravagant variety and confusion of mid-century decoration needed bringing into some sort of order. If there were to be more trained designers, then there had to be definite ways of teaching them; and that would require sound principles and general rules.

The illustration that opens Owen Jones *The Grammar of Ornament* (1856) is one of those examples that serve decades of argument; like Plato's cave and Adam Smith's pins, the theme of 'savage' body decoration comes back time and time again in the discourse of decoration. It is used by Adolf Loos in 1908 to bring the discourse to its close. In *The Grammar* tattooed decoration is described as 'an admirable lesson in composition'.

Jones describes modern decoration as enfeebled, but 'the ornament of a savage tribe, being the result of a natural instinct, is necessarily always true to its purpose...the beautiful New Zealand paddle would rival works of the highest civilisation'. Since

Jones bases the whole of his huge and beautiful book on the premise that decoration is a defining characteristic of a culture, then he is coming close to saying that 'savage tribes' can be the cultural superiors of nineteenth-century Britons. This is the earliest example of such an argument, and looks forward to the 'primitivism' of early twentieth-century artists such as Picasso and Brancusi.

His aim was to arrive at universal and teachable laws by studying all the known examples of decorative style. His method was not unlike that of the comparative botanist who collects and orders a mass of particular examples, and from them deduces general principles. Not surprisingly, he arrives at conclusions modelled on the life sciences. 'Whenever a style of ornament commands universal admiration, it will always be found to be in accordance with laws which regulate the distribution of form in nature.' He concludes that a student must be 'fully impressed with the law of the universal fitness of things in nature, with the wonderful variety of form, yet all arranged around some few fixed laws. . . . etc.' Such a concept of design can take its examples from anywhere, equally; there is no necessary reliance on precedents, and it is in principal ahistoric. Nothing less like Pugin's love of history and Christian association can be conceived. Jones elsewhere described the Gothic Revival as 'an attempt to galvanise a corpse'. His belief that a new approach to decoration could lead to a new style of architecture had a significant implication. The humble pattern designer could be elevated by it to the top of the pyramid of artistic status. Thus decoration could become a form of avant-gardism.

Jones had an extensive design practice, and took on work ranging from book design to massive projects such as this combined exhibition hall and transport interchange station in Paris. His largest completed commission was the interior painting of the Crystal Palace in 1851, which gained him an international reputation. He was also involved in the rebuilding of the Palace in south London, and in a similar scheme in Muswell Hill which came to nothing. Another project was to roof over Leicester Square. Amongst his many smaller interior designs were those for expensive shops and arcades in central London.

The juxtaposition of 'primitivism' with the most advanced levels of technology, capital and retailing are a characteristic of that aspect of modernism which Jones was the first to exemplify.

The *Grammar of Ornament* represents the extension of the cognitive monopoly of science into the arts, and fatally disrupts the values of traditional European culture by giving equal attention to everything it surveys. The very existence of such a compendium demonstrates that the cultural continuity of Europe was unravelling. The book must be reckoned one of the founding documents of aggressive modernism; it was distributed by the Department of Science and Art to all the Schools of Design in Great Britain and Ireland, and soon found its way to continental Europe and the United States.

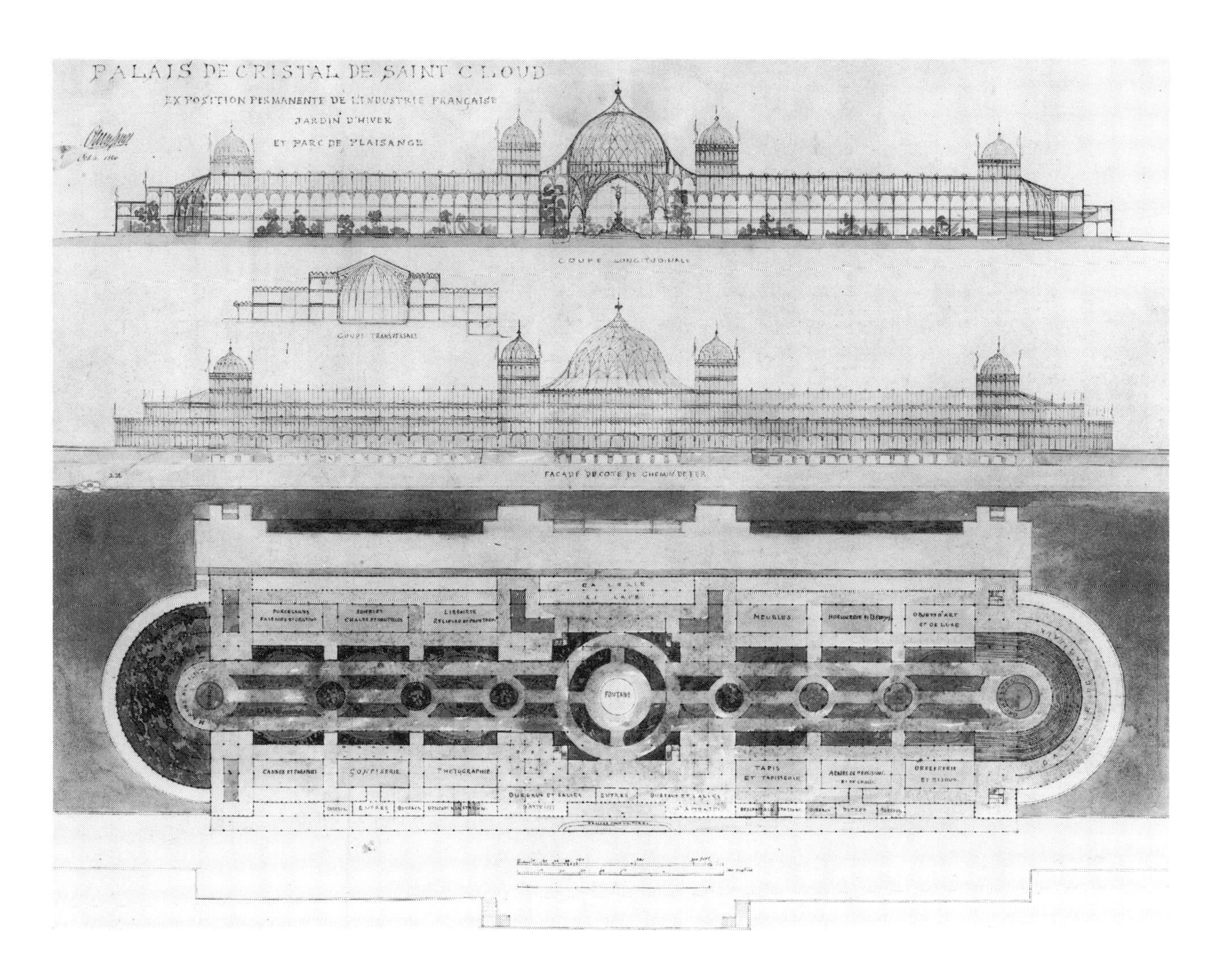

b) Owen Jones: plan, elevation and section of a permanent exhibition of French industry, in iron and glass, proposed for a site at St Cloud, Paris, 1860. (Coll. Victoria & Albert Museum).

Sample 8

Ruskin's own drawings and watercolours are exemplary of what he expected of the decorative artist, executed with a wonderfully light and tender hand. But his idea of an 'infantine' sight, in which the world appears as no more than ' an arrangement of patches of different colours, variously shaded' (*The Elements of Drawing* p.xv.) has been described as the 'explosive charge which was to blow the academic edifice sky-high' (Gombrich, 1968, p.12). By proposing 'natural facts' as his fundamental category, Ruskin's theory cuts through real history and academic precedent as surely as Jones' scientism.

a) A Dead Pheasant; John Ruskin, watercolour 13" x 20". (Coll. Victoria & Albert Museum).

Drawing is an integral part of designing; indeed, the two words used to mean much the same. Drawing is also a fundamental form of understanding that makes assumptions about the nature of reality, and these assumptions carry over into the completed work. Around the middle of the last century, there developed a sustained and vitriolic dispute about the kind of drawing required for decorative design, and, by extension, the kind of drawing that should be taught in schools and in the government-sponsored Schools of Design. The dispute between John Ruskin and Christopher Dresser can be taken as typical.

Ruskin's argument - developed in many writings but chiefly in *The Two Paths* (1857) - was essentially academic in one respect: that quality in the fine arts guaranteed quality in the decorative arts. Drawing, according to this theory, is the pursuit of the 'higher knowledge' of form which great art embodies and which must pass down from thence into ornament. But drawing must begin with what Ruskin calls 'natural facts'. These are given us through perception alone, unmediated by cultural conventions or scientific understanding; '...in

b) A coronet of leaves and acorns; John Ruskin, 1856, pencil and ink 3.3 cm. x 7.6 cm. This tiny drawing represents the next stage in Ruskin's process of design; the natural elements are being arranged in such a way that a stone-carver or silversmith might begin to work from them. See, for example, the carvings in the University Museum, Oxford, sample 9. (Coll. Victoria & Albert Museum).

representing this organic nature, Art has nothing to do with structures, causes or absolute facts; but only with appearance . . . . the artist has no concern with invisible structures, organic or inorganic.' *The Eagle's Nest* (1872).

On the other hand, Christopher Dresser asserted that 'a truthful figuration of principle as well as form must be given...the views which (the decorative designer) will generally have to give will be those that coincide with the architects plan of the building. . . . For ornamental purposes we deem literal copies altogether insufficient; representation of a more rigid and analytic character being necessary.' (Dresser, 1857, p.17ff). The Department of Science and Art called for designers to have 'a scientific comprehension of the world' (Forbes,1851), and brought the leading botanists of the day to lecture to the Schools of Design. Thus all decorative designers were to have a knowledge of Jones' 'laws that govern the distribution of form in nature'. In time, this came to be known as 'art-botany'. (See sample 15).

The distinction also relates to the issue of industrial production; the hard and unshaded outline drawing taught in the Schools of Design was thought to be most suitable for interpretation by loom-setters, mould-makers and other skilled workmen. Thus the style of drawing was also an index of the division of labour. Ruskin, on the other hand, believed that the tenderness required in a careful delineation of 'natural fact' passed over through the hand of the artist-craftsman into the finished work.

Two paths; two cultures. This is a fundamental division, a cleft or fault line running right through nineteenth century belief.

c

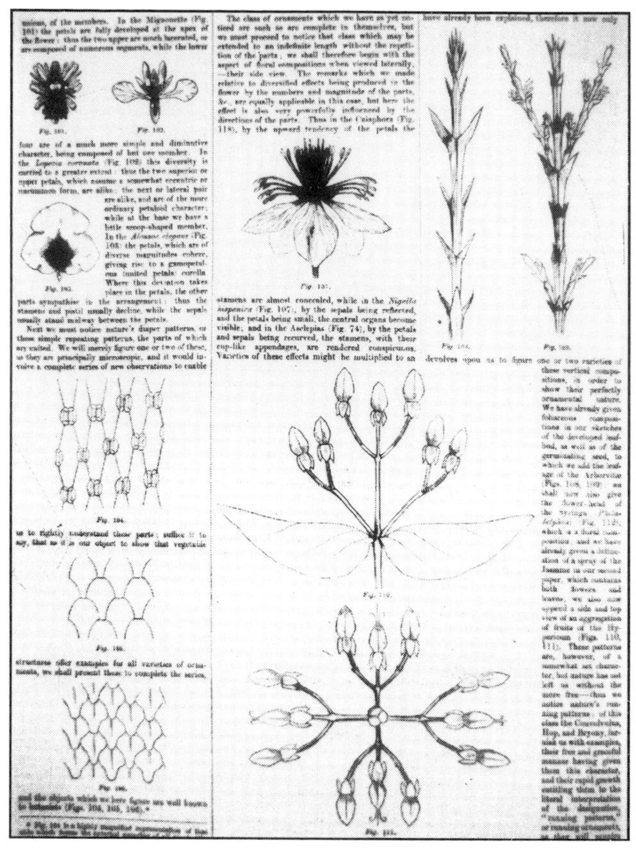

unions, of the members. In the Mignonette (Fig. 101) the petals are fully developed at the apex of the flower: thus the two upper are much lacerated, or are composed of numerous segments, while the lower four are of a much more simple and diminutive character, being composed of but one member. In the *Lopezia coronata* (Fig. 102) this diversity is carried to a greater extent: thus the two superior or upper petals, which assume a somewhat eccentric or acuminate form, are alike; the next or lateral pair are alike, and are of the more ordinary petaloid character; while at the base we have a little scoop-shaped member. In the *Alonsoa elegans* (Fig. 103) the petals, which are of diverse magnitudes cohere, giving rise to a gamopetalous (united petals) corolla. Where this deviation takes place in the petals, the other parts sympathise in the arrangement: thus the stamens and pistil usually decline, while the sepals usually stand midway between the petals.

Next we must notice nature's diaper patterns, or those simple repeating patterns, the parts of which are united. We will merely figure one or two of these, as they are principally microscopic, and it would involve a complete series of new observations to enable us to rightly understand these parts; suffice it to say, that as it is our object to show that vegetable structures offer examples for all varieties of ornaments, we shall present these to complete the series, and the objects which we here figure are well known to botanists (Figs. 104, 105, 106).*

The class of ornaments which we have as yet noticed are such as are complete in themselves, but we must proceed to notice that class which may be extended to an indefinite length without the repetition of the parts; we shall therefore begin with the aspect of floral compositions when viewed laterally,—their side view. The remarks which we made relative to diversified effects being produced in the flower by the numbers and magnitude of the parts, &c., are equally applicable in this case, but here the effect is also very powerfully influenced by the directions of the parts. Thus in the Cuisphora (Fig. 118), by the upward tendency of the petals the stamens are almost concealed, while in the *Nigella hispanica* (Fig. 107), by the sepals being reflected, and the petals being small, the central organs become visible; and in the Asclepias (Fig. 74), by the petals and sepals being recurved, the stamens, with their cup-like appendages, are rendered conspicuous. Varieties of these effects might be multiplied to an [illegible] have already been explained, therefore it now only devolves upon us to figure one or two varieties of these vertical compositions, in order to show their perfectly ornamental nature. We have already given foliaceous compositions in our sketches of the developed leaf-bud, as well as of the germinating seed, to which we add the leafage of the Arborvitae (Figs. 108, 109); we shall now also give the flower-head of the Syringa (*Philadelphus*) (Fig. 112), which is a floral composition; and we have already given a delineation of a spray of the Jasmine in our second paper, which contains both flowers and leaves, we also now append a side and top view of an aggregation of fruits of the Hypericum (Figs. 110, 111). These patterns are, however, of a somewhat set character, but nature has not left us without the more free—thus we notice nature's running patterns; of this class the Convolvulus, Hop, and Bryony, furnish us with examples, their free and graceful manner having given them this character, and their rapid growth entitling them to the literal interpretation of the designation, "running patterns," or running ornaments, [illegible]

Fig. 101. Fig. 102. Fig. 103. Fig. 104. Fig. 105. Fig. 106. Fig. 107. Fig. 108. Fig. 109. Fig. 110. Fig. 111.

c) Page from 'Botany as Adapted to Arts and Art Manufacturing'; an article in *The Art Journal* by Christopher Dresser, 1857. Dresser took exactly the opposite view to Ruskin: 'The artist must acquire at least an elementary knowledge of botany . . . for without this knowledge it is impossible to see objects. . . we do not accurately see objects until we understand them. . .' (Dresser, 1857).

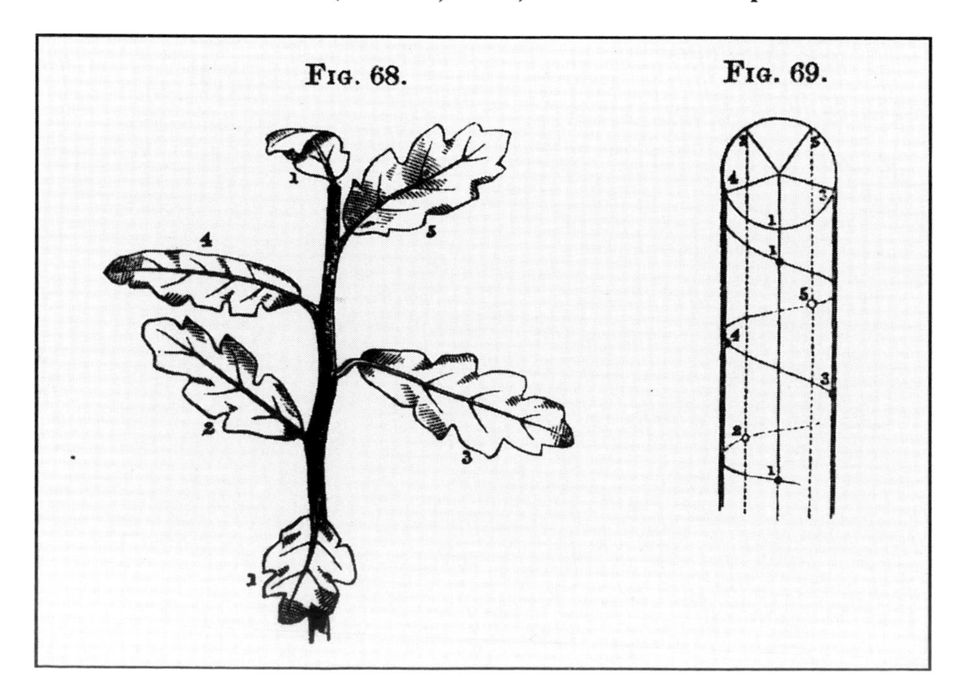

d

d) Illustrations from *The Art of Decorative Design* by Christopher Dresser, 1862. Dresser was an eminent botanist at a the time when the main tool of the science became the microscope. It was not simply the visible architecture of the plant and its symmetries that were to be delineated, but its invisible structures of cell and membrane. These together would provide a visual language for the new epoch of science, industry and art. This illustration was also used in one of his books on botany.

Sample 9

Sometimes we can find examples that exactly sum up these differences. Buildings are not as pure as ideas and their final condition is always the result of compromises; yet, taking careful account of this, useful comparisons can be made.

The University Museum at Oxford, inspired by Ruskin's ideas and example, was designed by the Dublin firm of Deane and Woodward, with carvings by the O'Shea brothers. Ruskin hoped the completed building would be exemplary, not only housing botanical and zoological specimens but showing, in its naturalistic decoration, how such examples could be used for design. It would, in effect, embody the idea of a qualitative and Christian science. The capital and base of each column is carved with a different and exactly rendered floral, leaf or seed motif; the shaft of each column is of a different polished stone, to provide a geological reference library. The 'natural' detail is carried right down to the smallest

a

a) and b) Interior details of the University Museum, Oxford, 1855-68. Architects; Mssrs Deane and Woodward; carving by Michael O'Shea. (Photo; Barbara Freeman).

b

c) Interior detail, Philadelphia Academy of Fine Arts, 1871-76. Architect; Frank Furness, with George Hewitt. See also the cover of this book, and frontispiece. (Photo; Barbara Freeman).

details of brassware and door handles, in direct paraphrase of the early Gothic that Ruskin so much admired. (For the sort of drawing he expected, see sample 8).

Frank Furness's decoration, however, is a transatlantic culmination of the opposing 'South Kensington school'. Furness and his partner George Hewitt were well aware of the work of Jones and Dresser. 'In several preserved drawings, flowers are rendered in "plan" and "elevation"showing their geometric symmetry like the working drawings of a building.' (O'Gorman, 1973, p.35). When this manner of drawing was applied to architectural decoration, and made by mechanical methods rather than hand-wrought, the result was something halfway between mechanised vegetation and organic mechanism. There is something in this building that can be called a 'machine aesthetic'. In place of Ruskinian variability and naturalism there is uniformity, precision, and abstraction. This is seen to advantage in the low relief carving and moulding of the entrance hall (see frontispiece).

Both buildings are highly self-conscious cultural statements and they can be taken as representative of the two antithetical tendencies. From today's viewpoint it would be easy to see the first as antiquarian and the second as proto-modernist. But that is too simple. The University Museum was built to house modern, even avant-garde activities and to bring science into the university curriculum. Charles Eastlake described the decorations as 'tentative. They represent one of the earliest departures from the beaten track of architectural design.' (Eastlake, 1872, p.286). The construction of the central hall of the building was in the most modern wrought iron and glass. The Philadelphia Academy, on the other hand, was to house a cultural tradition, and is - decoration excepted - a fairly conventional structure.

In the clash between these two approaches to contemporary design we catch sight of a deep division within the institutions of the times, perhaps even a struggle for mastery.

d) Interior detail, Philadelphia Academy of Fine Arts, 1871-76. Architect; Frank Furness, with George Hewitt. See also the cover of this book, and frontispiece. (Photo; Barbara Freeman).

Sample 10

The purpose of the last comparison was to make the differences vivid; but in their day they were part of the general variety of mid-century life. Walking to work each day through the centre of Belfast I pass similar antithetical examples. . . .

a) **Detail of a building in Bedford Place, Belfast. (Photo; the author).**

This is a good, though rather plain example of 'conventional' ornament applied to the exterior of a building; in the United States, this would be called the 'Eastlake Style', after Charles of that name, whose writings on design transmitted many British ideas across the Atlantic. This work would have been carved by mechanical routers, which came into use in the 1840s, and began to supercede hand-carving in the 1850s whenever simple geometric motifs were specified. Indeed, the demand for simple geometry and the sort of pattern drawing that it required, is clearly implicated in the adoption of such new devices. Something of the effects of wood-working machinery may be seen in the furniture which Eastlake designed in the 1860s.

b) Illustration from Eastlake *Hints on Household Taste*,(1872 ed., p.131).

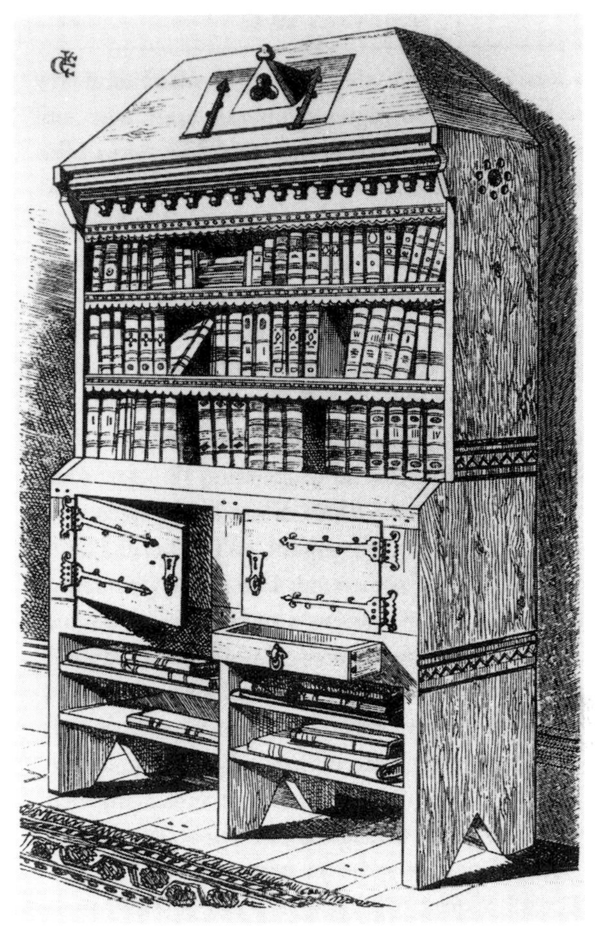

This is a detail of the porch to a fine polychrome brick office building. There is something in the quality of this carving that suggests it may be by the O'Shea brothers - although there was a notable group of architectural sculptors at work in Belfast in the mid-century. The building itself has been described as 'Ruskinian' or as being 'in the style of Woodward'. In fact it was designed by W.H. Lynn who was also an important figure in the Celtic Revival whilst at the same time remodelling old castles into French chateaux and designing neo-medieval city walls for Quebec.

Contrasts such as this can be seen all over our city centres, and are the everyday traces of the extremes represented in Philadelphia and Oxford.

c) Detail of a building in May Street, Belfast. (Photo; the author)

Sample 11

'The quasi-fidelity with which the forms of a rose, or a bunch of ribbons, or a ruined castle, can be reproduced on carpets, crockery and wall-papers will always possess a certain kind of charm for the uneducated eye...' Charles Eastlake *Hints on Household Taste* (3rd ed., 1872).

Twenty years after Dickens' Government Inspector had upbraided Sissy Jupe for preferring 'pictures of what was very pretty', Charles Eastlake was still struggling to persuade the people 'to be a people of Fact, and of nothing but Fact.' These examples would have made his heart sink. The first was designed for a nursery. The second appears to have been printed for a gentleman's games room: observe the faithful servants, and the Highland costume.

We have to be wary of dismissing such designs as 'kitsch'. In their day they were popular for quite definite reasons. Kate Greenaway's designs, in particular, became famous because they evidently catered for a taste that was both advanced and nostalgic: her female figures refer back to a pre-industrial England, but they are also recognisably dressed in an informal 'aesthetic' manner.

a) Wallpaper by Kate Greenaway, entitled 'The Seasons'; printed by D. Walker, 1893. (Coll. Victoria & Albert Museum).

The Highland scenes are also part of the construction of pseudo-histories through taste - in this case, that of 'Highland culture' as a commodity available to tourists and the owners of country estates (see sample 18). Designs such as these were rooted in real preoccupations and commitments, even if these now appear to be essentially spurious and 'retardaire'.

The popularity of pictorial pattern and naturalistic ornament could not be expunged, despite all propaganda to the contrary. What seems to have happened was that it went 'downmarket' except in those locations such as clubs, sporting situations and nurseries, spaces in which the particular functions had to be signified. And this is still, with some very expensive exceptions, a general rule. Kate Greenaway's designs set in motion a stream of copies and paraphrases, and cheaper modern versions of these sporting scenes can be found in any major store today. This is partly a matter of class differences. As the French sociologist, Pierre Bourdieu, observes 'Popular naturalism recognizes beauty in the image of a beautiful thing.... Nothing is more alien to popular consciousness than the idea of an aesthetic pleasure that, to put it in Kantian terms, is independent of the charming of the senses' (see Postscript).

The expensive exceptions were, and remain, prints made in direct and learned paraphrase of eighteenth-century chintz patterns; these have remained a staple of the more expensive trade since their inception.

b) Pictorial wallpaper, c. 1870. (Coll. Victoria & Albert Museum).

Sample 12

Edgar Allan Poe's *The Philosophy of Furniture* (1840) preached an interior decoration without any form of representation at all. 'Touching pattern...distinct grounds, and vivid circular or cycloid features, of no meaning, are here Median laws. The abomination of flowers, or representations of well-known objects of any kind, should not be endured within the limits of Christendom'. Carpets and wall coverings should be 'arabesque'. By 'no meaning', Poe clearly meant 'without picturing'; but the question of what abstract, flat pattern signified if it had no pictorial or emblematic aspect was a question that demanded an answer.

For Owen Jones and his associates, pictures and emblems were replaced by ideas of 'harmony' and 'symmetry' from which an 'aesthetic' ornament can be created. 'We may term those styles symbolic in which ordinary elements have been chosen for the sake of their significations ..(but)..Those that are composed of elements devised solely from principals of symmetry of form and harmony of colour, and exclusively for their effect on our perception of the beautiful, without any further extraneous or ulterior aim, may be termed aesthetic.' (Ralph Wornum, 1855). The meaning of such a pattern lay in its effect on our perception of the beautiful. The relations between figure-motif and ground were to be 'harmonious'; that is, the space was to be shallow and the relations between figure and ground were to be defined by colour as much as by shape, thus creating patterns in which figure and ground were almost indistinguishable.

Designs such as these examples by Owen Jones from the 1870s attempt a direct communication between the eye and the understanding, without narrative, pictorial or emblematic-symbolic transactions. This, unmistakably, is an argument for an abstract painting; for what Christopher Dresser later came to call 'an art wholly of mental origin', which would be superior to pictorial imagery by virtue of the unity between means and ends. The concept of an art whose meaning lies solely in our perception of the beautiful is an idea ultimately deriving from Immanuel Kant's *Critique of Judgement*, and thus it is seeking to transmit to the decorative arts a superior - because 'disinterested' - aesthetic status. By such means, decoration might become an avant-garde art for art's sake.

Owen Jones, as theorist, teacher, interior and surface designer and creator of *The Grammar of Ornament* might be called the first self-conscous modernist of decoration. His imagination has been described as 'abstract, conceptual and experimental' (Darby, 1974). In his circle, arguments about decoration were conducted in terms that look forward to the twentieth century and, finally and logically, to the abandonment of decoration altogether.

a) and b) Wallpapers designed by Owen Jones for the firm of Jeffrey and Co., 1874. (Coll. Victoria & Albert Museum).

a

b

Sample 13

If we take Owen Jones and Christopher Dresser as the most typical figures of 'normative' design, then William Morris, as Ruskin's follower, may be taken to be their 'critical' counterpart. But this would be too simple. Morris is universally regarded as a great pattern designer, but usually discussed and criticised within the terms of the arguments he himself set up - those of the Arts and Crafts Movement. These stressed the 'traditional' and 'craft' aspect of his work, and the 'natural' derivation of his patterns. But now we should see these designs as caught up in the whole discourse of decoration. This makes them less original but more central.

His mature designs are pictorial enough for us to recognise the flowers from which they derive, but the stems of the pattern follow geometrical rather than botanical rules. Furthermore, the space that the pattern creates, though not flat, is not in recessional perspective; most typically it is a layered space with an interweaving rhythm whereby pattern elements 'below' come up and over the 'upper' elements. These two or more layers float above or are interpenetrated by a ground which does not lead the eye 'back' into the space but maintains a gentle tension between the different layers. Seen on a real wall, from shifting positions and in varying light, the patterns set up a remarkable counterpoint and colour mix, creating effects like those to be found in post-impressionist painting. Modern reproductions, with glossy inks on hard papers, cannot match the softness of the originals which maintain their colour balance even when they fade. This constructional approach to pattern may relate to Morris's experience of weaving, but in the terms under discussion here it is a middle way between the extremes of 'fact' and 'fancy'.

However, Morris's own theory of the meaning of his patterns is a restatement of the English 'picturesque' and of Ruskinian naturalism: 'You may be sure that any decoration is futile, and has fallen into at least the first stage of degradation, when it does not remind you of something beyond itself, of something of which it is a visible symbol . . . I, as a Western man and a picture lover, must still insist on plenty of meaning in your patterns...those natural forms which are at once most familiar and most delightful to us, as well as from association as from beauty, are best for our purpose.'

The knowledge that these patterns were designed to be printed by manual rather than machine methods, and that the colours were, at least in principle, 'natural' adds another layer of meaning. It is not simply a pattern that you were buying, but a critical attitude to the present. There is an implied purity and simplicity of intention on behalf of both designer and client.

a) 'Chrysanthemum' wallpaper by Wm. Morris, 1877. (Coll. Victoria & Albert Museum).

b) 'Myrtle' wallpaper by Wm. Morris, 1889. (Coll. Victoria & Albert Museum).

a

b

Sample 14

a) The 'Arab Hall' in Lord Leighton's house, South Kensigton, London, 1864. (Photo; Leighton House Museum).

The desire for a unified style could be met through the self-conscious simplicity of Morris, or through the thorough and learned synthesis of Alexander Thomson; but it was also possible to achieve a form of unity through ingenious assemblage.

The ambition to synthesise general and normative rules for decoration by surveying the whole of known culture is more easily reached in the pages of a book than in any working practice. At first it could hardly do more than promote an extreme aesthetic eclecticism in which items, motifs and patterns could be brought together 'exclusively for their effect on our perception of the beautiful'. Unity was achieved by careful selection and combination - a process which took no regard of the original significance of the components.

Such was the interior of the house that the painter Frederick Leighton had built in 1864, designed by George Aitchison but with later additions by several others. In time the house became a collage of styles, which included an 'Arab Hall' faced internally with a gorgeous array of real Islamic tiles that Leighton had collected in his journeys, and with neo-Islamic details by certain of his contemporaries (notably Walter Crane).

b) 'Collage' of islamic tiles in the 'Arab Hall'. (Photo; Barbara Freeman).

The central space of the house was treated in deep blue tiles by William de Morgan, and the rest of the building was a sumptuous display of *objets d'art*, wallpapers, furnishings and textiles, housing a fine collection of paintings. While this assemblage was too individual to be fitted into any one 'style' it is often mentioned in the literature on the Aesthetic Movement, and it is useful to think of Leighton's interiors as a 'clearing house' of decorative ideas and influences - in this case, 'Oriental'. The neo-Islamic element in Victorian decoration is usually underplayed and understudied. Its abstraction fitted well both with normative ideas and with the vogue for 'Venetian Gothic'. Many lavish and learned books were published on the subject; but Leighton's interest was that of the aesthete, not the scholar. He mixed motifs and patterns from different regions and epochs on the basis of their appearance alone, thereby assigning them a new meaning. By amalgamating the original with the contemporary in a collage of differences, he was synthesising a new reality. This all-gathering aestheticism is the artistic face of imperial rapacity. 'It is, above all, a discourse that... is produced and exists in an uneven exchange with various kinds of power... it is, rather than expresses, a certain will or intention to understand, in some cases to control, manipulate, even appropriate what is a manifestly different... world.' (Said, 1978, p.12).

c) Detail from the 'Arab Hall'. (Photo; Barbara Freeman).

The creation of a richly decorated and exotic interior came to stand as a metaphor for a fashioning of the inner life. This is perhaps more easily seen in the writings of French Symbolism, rather than in the designs themselves. This was a literature with which Leighton was well acquainted, and it includes J.K. Huysmans *Against Nature* (1884) and the writings of the Goncourt brothers. In *Against Nature* (A Rebours), the hero, des Esseintes, constructs for himself a series of exquisitely fashioned interiors within which to meditate on pleasure and seek relief from the insistent ugliness and falsity of Parisian life. This is what Maurice Barrès, writing in his *Culte de Moi* (1889), described as 'materialising the outward forms of my sensibilities'; 'Our morality, our religion, our sense of nationality are crumbling things from which, I opine, we can derive no rules of life.... we must hold ourselves to that reality of Self....We must defend it each day and each day create it afresh...it is we who create the universe.' (ibid. pp.14-21).

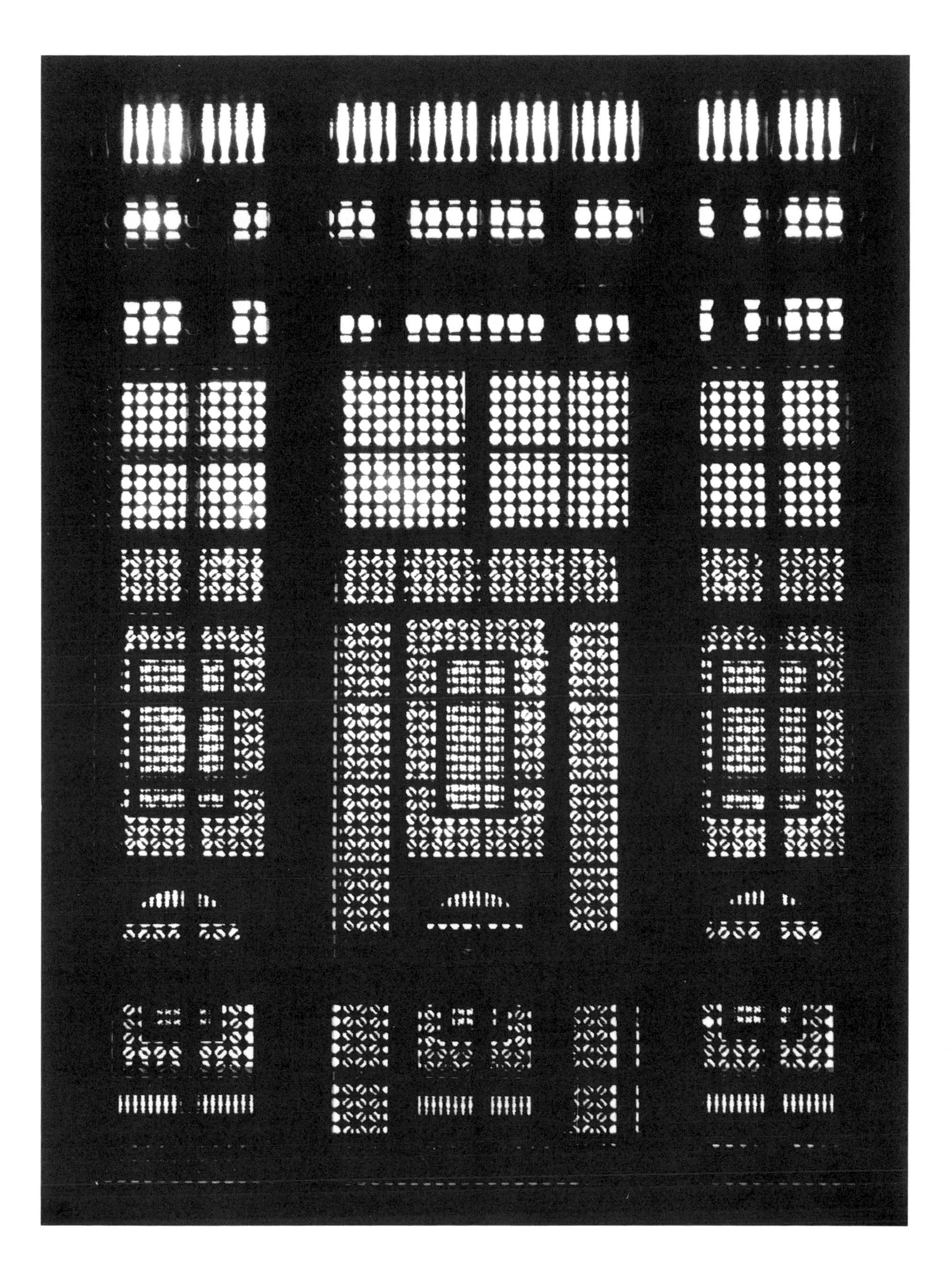

d) 'Zenana' shutters in the 'Arab Hall'.
(Photo; Barbara Freeman).

Sample 15 (A)

But assemblage and collage are merely a stage on the way to a truly unified and modern decoration. The way to this objective could not lie through an emblematic expression of beliefs - such as Pugin had attempted - still less through pictoriality. 'We cannot hope that symbolism will again prevail. . . . What must find utterance in a national system of decoration is our secular knowledge - our knowledge of nature as revealed to us through the sciences, and of refinement' (C. Dresser, 1862). The content of decoration will be 'mind' and the source of motifs will be 'secular knowledge'; i.e. art-botany, or 'decorative forms (that) express thoughts, feelings and ideas without the aid of recognized symbols'. Such creation of abstract motifs, which Dresser half-humorously describes in terms of rising and falling vectors, are linked analogically to musical composition and to the creation of meaning through melodic transformations.

'The existence of a deeper unity between form and sound might be expected in view of many considerations. A fiddle bow drawn across the edge of a sheet of glass on which sand has been sprinkled, while giving rise to an audible sound, causes the particles of sand to collect in given shapes, which vary according to the note produced. . . . Our attention is here awakened to the existence of a similarity of music and ornament in the power they each possess of working upon the mind. . . the aesthetic arts are intimately related.' (Dresser, 1862, p.44).

'Those works which are most fully of mental origin. . . are those which are most noble. . . pictorial art can, in its highest development, only symbolize imagination or emotion by the representation of idealized reality (but) true ornamentation is of purely mental origin and consists of symbolized imagaination or emotion only. I therefore argue that ornamentation is not only a fine art. . . it is indeed a higher art than that practised by the pictorial artist, as it is wholly of mental origin.' (Dresser, 1870).

a) figure in text from Dresser's *The Art of Decorative Design* (1862).

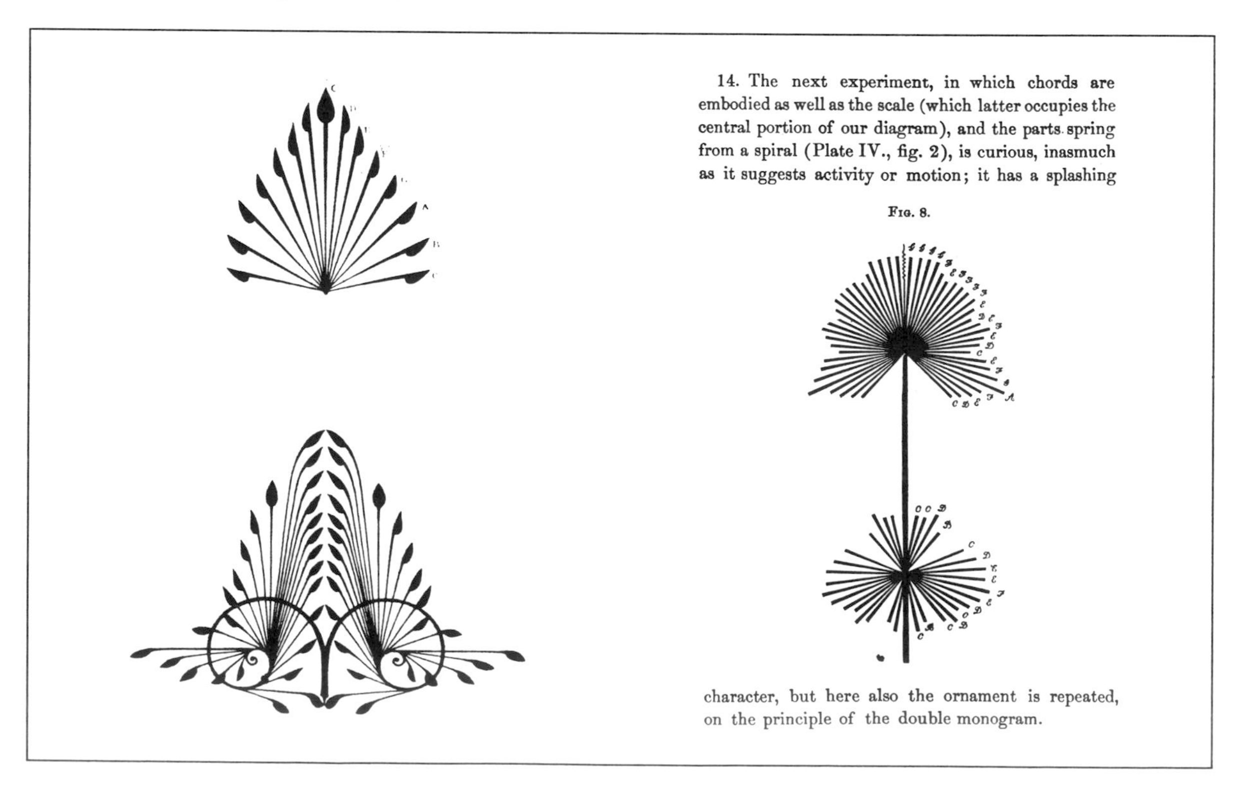
14. The next experiment, in which chords are embodied as well as the scale (which latter occupies the central portion of our diagram), and the parts spring from a spiral (Plate IV., fig. 2), is curious, inasmuch as it suggests activity or motion; it has a splashing

FIG. 8.

character, but here also the ornament is repeated, on the principle of the double monogram.

In the pages of *The Art of Decorative Design*, Christopher Dresser begins to work out the logical consequences of abstract decoration.

If he were alive today, we can be certain that he would have been intensely interested in visualisation techniques, fractal geometry and the use of the computer in design. His was a cast of mind that combined a positivist concept of science with a transcendental belief that there may be 'laws' of expression much like scientific 'laws'. It is an attitude common to all the successors of Owen Jones such as Dresser, Arthur Mackmurdo and Charles Voysey. Very similar ideas were being developed a little later in the United States, by Louis Sullivan.

Dresser's life was divided between botany and decoration, and he wrote as much on one as on the other. As a relentlessly busy professional designer he was willing to work in many ways, and his production is not always in perfect step with his theory.

Voysey summed up this new orthodoxy in the first issue of *The Studio* (1893) 'To go to nature is, of course, to go to the fountainhead; but before a living plant a man must go through an elaborate process of selection and analysis'. Natural forms have to be 'reduced to mere symbols'. If the artist does this 'although he has gone direct to Nature... he has become a true inventor ... we are at once relieved from restrictions of style and period and can live and work in the present with laws always revealing fresh possibilities.' What Voysey is sketching out here, is a generative system or shape-grammar. Such a system can always, in principle, be given an algebraic expression and therefore, finally, be mechanised.

b) Wallpaper by C. Dresser. (Coll. Victoria & Albert Museum).

The writings of Arthur Mackmurdo are likewise full of references to 'evolutionary tendencies', 'harmonizing laws' and 'that ordering of parts which the imagination discerns throughout nature'. Mackmurdo was a pupil of Herbert Spencer and Thomas Huxley; he regarded himself as having had a scientific education. For him, a design was 'a work of nature as a plant may be said to be a work of nature.' This identification of culture with the laws of the universe is the culmination of the normative tradition, and its ideological force is self-evident. It is the cosmological justification of late nineteenth-century modernism.

c) 'Cereus' wallpaper by C.F.A.Voysey, designed for W.Woolland and Co., c.1886 (Coll. Victoria & Albert Museum).

Sample 15 (B)

From the interview in *The Studio* quoted above one might have expected Voysey and his colleagues to have led British design into the twentieth century; but he was tied to a clientele and way of working that could look over into a new world but could not enter it. The refusal of the 'art nouveau' in favour of an Arts and Crafts tradition marks the retreat of English society into an 'ancien regime'. Thereafter, the discourse had to complete its trajectory elsewhere.

In the United States, the influence of the 'South Kensington school' was reinforced by French precepts and the desire to create a uniquely American and 'democratic' art that would be free from the hierarchical associations of the European tradition.

In Boston, the scholar and connoisseur Denman Ross imagined an 'art of pure design' as a discipline comparable to music and dancing. In *A Theory of Pure Design* (1907) and *On Drawing and Painting* (1912) he distinguished between 'two modes of drawing... the mode of pure design and the mode or representation'. He printed examples of motifs which he then inverts and varies into complicated 'phrases' and 'melodic lines'. At this point, decorative ideas pass over abstract painting.

In New York, the firm of Louis Tiffany began a professional and business relation with Christopher Dresser, of which one outcome was the development during the 1890s of Tiffany's famous 'favrile' glass, whose forms are the outcome of 'art-botanical' teaching.

In Chicago, Louis Sullivan developed a style of decorative drawing which likened the line growing from a point to the emergence of a stem from the seed. Thus emancipated from its past, a decorative line can take on enormous ambitions....

Fig. 215

Fig. 216

d) Figures in text, from Denman Ross, *A Theory of Pure Design* (1907).

'Man stands, by virtue of his powers, a solitary ego within a universe of energy; a witness, a participant; and by virtue of his powers a co-creator - his creations are but parallels of himself.' (Sullivan, 1924).

Sullivan was a pupil of Frank Furness and the teacher of Frank Lloyd Wright. There is a dynasty of ideas at work here which marks the movement of the positivist and utilitarian world of South Kensington toward a Nietzschean glorification of the creative spirit. Sullivan's designs and writings become the distillation of the inner meaning of 'art botany'; that when the works of Man have the necessity and unerring fitness of Nature, human perfection through progress will have been achieved. (see Menocal, 1981).

The organic analogies of Sullivan's 'doctrine of parallelism' went to form the architectural theory and practice of Wright. A study of Wright's work and the unity of structure and decoration that he sought and achieved, lies beyond the scope of this book. But it is interesting to consider his architecture, and other architectures of the twentieth century, as being as much an outcome of the discourse of decoration, as of strictly architectural traditions.

e) Louis Sullivan, relief ornament, Merchant's National Bank, Grinnell, Iowa, 1913. (Photo; the author).

Sample 16

'"And could a kitchen range ever be otherwise than ugly?" . . . Remember, it is not the humbleness of its purpose or the simplicity of its form which prevents it from being so. How many of us have peeped inside the threshold of a Welsh cottage or Devonshire farmhouse, and longed to sketch its comfortable chimney corner and ample hearth! Could we say as much for any basement room in Mayfair? And yet there was a time when no such difference existed between the appointments of town and country dwellings.' Charles Eastlake.

The intellectual vehemence of the normative strand of the discourse provoked an equal and opposite reaction. . . .

In the 1830s, writers on design thought in terms of a 'manufacturing population' amongst whom the principles of good design could be 'disseminated'; but by 1893, W.G. Collingwood could imagine 'an honest handful of tradesmen and farmers, and a decent lot of labouring men' who might sustain 'a spontaneous art instinct... (creating). . . domestic ornament of an unpretending but thoroughly artistic sort.. .. In secluded English villages... untaught genius has created native styles and schools of carving and pottery not unworthy of serious commendation.' In the intervening fifty years the nation had been transformed and a modern industrial state come

Farm house Fire-place,
Chambercombe, Devon.

a) Illustrated plate from C.F. Eastlake, *Hints on Household Taste* (1868) Farm house fire-place; Chambercombe, Devon.

into being. In opposition to Dresser's national style, founded on 'secular knowledge', Collingwood's critical view was that 'a real national style can only exist when the people produce it, and when the people enjoy it.' (Collingwood, 1893, p.208 etc.) But this qualitative concept of 'the people' is in the greatest possible contrast to the quantitative 'population'. The ideological collision between these two concepts has both benign and sinister aspects.

The rural ideal, with its nationalist assumptions, became the guiding principle of a great swathe of English society. Eastlake's praise of the rural kitchen, his aestheticisation of the farmhouse and assumption that town and country were long ago at one are significant stages in the creation of a taste for refined rusticity, as strong today as ever.

That industrial modernity eroded this supposed national 'character' had been noticed as early as 1851. Ralph Wornum, writing in the catalogue to the Great Exhibition, set an agenda for five decades of critical design and scholarship. 'The time has now gone by, at least in Europe, for the development of any particular or national style, and for this reason it is necessary to distinguish the various tastes that have prevailed through past ages, and preserve them as distinct expressions, or otherwise by using indiscriminately all materials, we should lose all expression. . . if all. . . is to degenerate into a uniform mixture of all elements, nothing will be beautiful.' The entire aporia of an industrial culture is embedded in this problem. Then, as now, the irresistible power of industry and capital to impose its own international uniformity provoked a demand for 'distinct' national expression and local 'character'. When this could not be found it had to be invented.

Eastlake's *Hints on Household Taste*, first published in 1868, was by far the best known and most widely read manual of its kind; it reached its third edition in 1872. But it was not the only one. During the 1870s and early 1880s a stream of similar publications appeared. Here are some titles:

M.J. Loftie, *The Dining Room*, London 1878
Mrs Orrinsmith, *The Drawing Room*, London 1878
Lady Barker, *The Bedroom and the Boudoir*, London 1878
Rhoda and Agnes Garret, *Suggestions for House Decoration*, London 1879
Mary Eliza Haweis, *The Art of Decoration*, London 1881
R.W. Edis, *Decoration and Furniture of Town Houses*, London 1881

To these should be added a number of new titles of women's magazines, of which the most famous or lasting were:

Weldon Ladies Journal (finally *Homes and Gardens*) from 1879
The Ladies Pictorial from 1881
The Ladies World (ed. Oscar Wilde) 1886-1890
The Housewife from 1886
Hearth and Home from 1891

These books and journals promoted an advanced but respectable taste, and mark a stage of development beyond the *Hints*. As we shall see in sample 20, they recommended Japanese design and the sparseness of decor that went with its adoption by the Aesthetic Movement. The existence of this literature suggests that the design reform movements initiated in the 1850s had now established themselves as an orthodoxy in which contrasting styles could be juxtaposed without incongruity. The publication of *The Studio* (from 1893) marked the assumption of the decorative and applied arts into the same status as fine art painting, sculpture and architecture.

DEVELOPMENT

OF

ORNAMENTAL ART

IN THE

INTERNATIONAL EXHIBITION:

BEING A CONCISE STATEMENT OF THE LAWS WHICH GOVERN THE PRODUCTION AND APPLICATION OF ORNAMENT, WITH REFERENCES TO THE BEST EXAMPLES.

BY

C. DRESSER, PH.D., F.L.S.

ETC. ETC.

DAY AND SON, LITHOGRAPHERS TO THE QUEEN,
6, GATE STREET, LINCOLN'S INN FIELDS, & PROCESSES COURT,
INTERNATIONAL EXHIBITION, LONDON.
1862.

HINTS

ON

HOUSEHOLD TASTE

IN

FURNITURE, UPHOLSTERY

AND OTHER DETAILS

BY

CHARLES L. EASTLAKE

F.R.I.B.A., ARCHITECT

AUTHOR OF 'A HISTORY OF THE GOTHIC REVIVAL'

'Parmi ces splendeurs à bon marché, ce faux goût et ce faux luxe, nous sommes ravis quand nous trouvons un banc bien fait, une bonne table de chêne portant d'aplomb sur ses pieds, des rideaux de laine qui paraissent être en laine, une chaise commode et solide, une armoire qui s'ouvre et se ferme bien, nous montrant en dedans et en dehors le bois dont elle est fait, et laissant deviner son usage. Espérons un retour vers ces idées saines, et qu'en fait de mobilier, comme en toute chose, on en viendra à comprendre que le goût consiste à paraître ce que l'on est et non ce que l'on voudrait être'
VIOLLET-LE-DUC

THIRD EDITION

(REVISED)

LONDON
LONGMANS, GREEN, AND CO.
1872

DECORATION & FURNITURE

OF

TOWN HOUSES

A SERIES OF CANTOR LECTURES DELIVERED BEFORE THE SOCIETY OF ARTS, 1880, AMPLIFIED AND ENLARGED

BY

ROBERT W. EDIS, F.S.A. F.R.I.B.A.

ARCHITECT

WITH 29 FULL-PAGE ILLUSTRATIONS AND NUMEROUS SKETCHES

SECOND EDITION

LONDON
C. KEGAN PAUL & CO., 1 PATERNOSTER SQUARE
1881

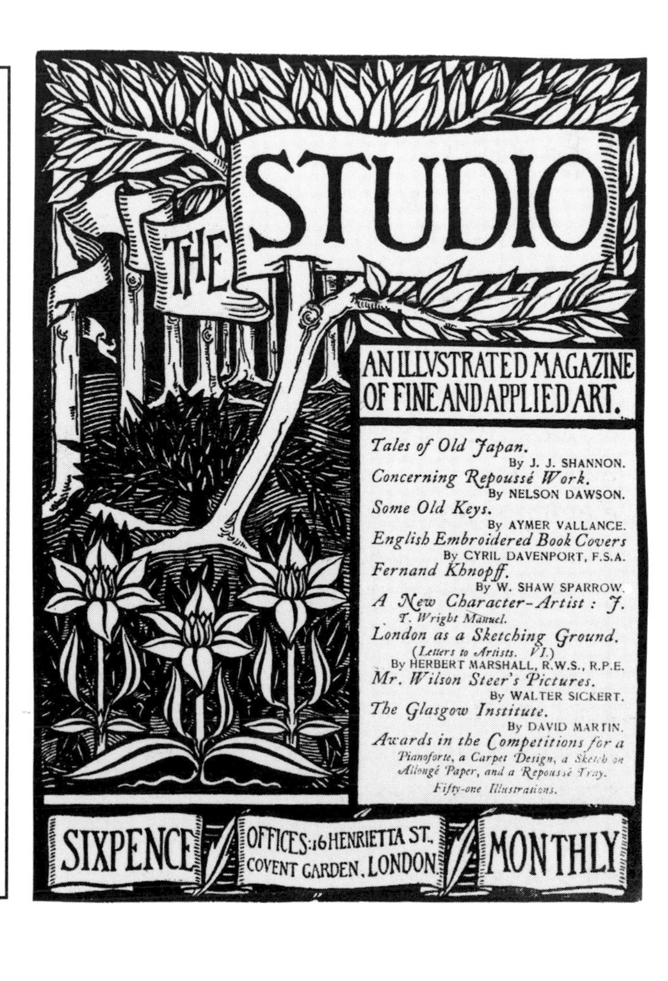

THE STUDIO

AN ILLVSTRATED MAGAZINE OF FINE AND APPLIED ART.

Tales of Old Japan. By J. J. SHANNON.
Concerning Repoussé Work. By NELSON DAWSON.
Some Old Keys. By AYMER VALLANCE.
English Embroidered Book Covers By CYRIL DAVENPORT, F.S.A.
Fernand Khnopff. By W. SHAW SPARROW.
A New Character-Artist: J. T. Wright Manuel.
London as a Sketching Ground. (*Letters to Artists. VI.*) By HERBERT MARSHALL, R.W.S., R.P.E.
Mr. Wilson Steer's Pictures. By WALTER SICKERT.
The Glasgow Institute. By DAVID MARTIN.
Awards in the Competitions for a Pianoforte, a Carpet Design, a Sketch on Allongé Paper, and a Repoussé Tray.
Fifty-one Illustrations.

SIXPENCE OFFICES: 16 HENRIETTA ST. COVENT GARDEN. LONDON MONTHLY

Sample 17

The critical wing of the discourse of decoration became steadily more preoccupied with the idea of 'distinct expression' and 'the people' as the century progressed.

Morris's search was for a putative English 'character', not style. The idea of 'character' implied a natural and authentic quality, whereas 'style' signified artifice. His business manager, Warrington Taylor, wrote in his letters 'You don't want any style, you want something English in character' and 'the test of good work would be absence of style'. This implied, however, a view of 'English' that was highly selective.

'Everything English, except stockjobbing London and cotton Manchester, is essentially small, and of a homely farmhouse kind of poetry...above all things nationality is the greatest social trait, English Gothic is small as our landscape is small, it is sweet picturesque homely farmyardish....' (Warrington Taylor, 1862, quoted in Girouard, 1977, p.18).

There was no clearly identifiable 'national' model to which Morris could look for an ideal prototype. The English vernacular was a complicated plurality, quickly responsive to commercial pressures and imported fashions, and lacking a consistent symbology. Any origins it had in a supposed 'folk' art had long ago been lost. The seventeenth- and eighteenth-century workshops, whose design methods Morris was attempting to emulate, were always open to foreign and even exotic material, transforming them as they arrived. These exotica had always included the 'moorish' and 'oriental' influences against which Morris, in his theory, was committed to struggle, but which in his practice he was eager to absorb.

Here he is, reinventing eighteenth-century chintz patterns for late nineteenth-century wallpaper and implicitly reinventing a golden age of English design, before the factory system. The lack of commitment to industry and advanced technology, which some historians have seen as a leading characteristic of British society, is revealed in the decorative arts and in domestic architecture more vividly then anywhere else.

The preoccupation with 'distinct expression' and 'the people' was, from the start, ideologically ambivalent; it was an association that could belong equally to left or right. In the forlorn conditions prevailing after the Great War, the idea of a national character became capable of sinister development.

a) 'Wild Tulip' wallpaper by Wm. Morris, 1884. (Coll. Victoria & Albert Museum).

b) 'Bird and Anemone' wallpaper by Wm. Morris, 1882. (Coll. Victoria & Albert Museum).

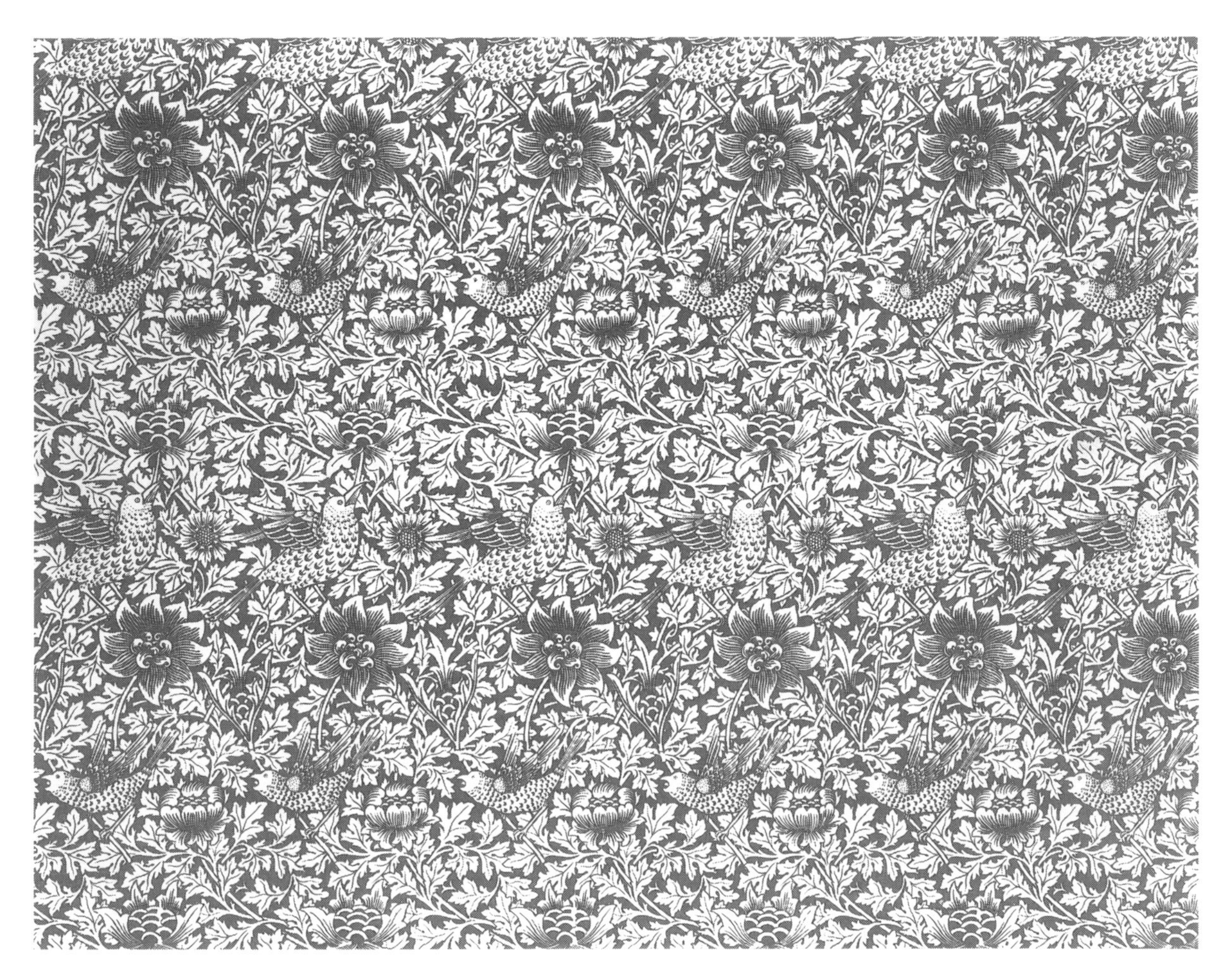

Sample 18

The desire to preserve 'distinct expression' stimulated the serious study of cultural difference. It made designers and clients acutely conscious of national and local characteristics of style. Here the 'distinct expressions' could meet with romantic nationalism and be glorified as 'traditions'. These should not be thought of as anti-modern tendencies in any simple sense, since it was through romantic nationalism that modern Europe was created. What we are looking at are competing versions of what it meant to become modern, and different strategies for dealing with the shock of it.

Within the British Isles the assertion of national differences led to some curious results, since 'real' differences (in so far as they had ever coherently existed) had been severely eroded before the century began. Distinct expression had to be constructed, sometimes on the basis of very little evidence indeed. Nor was there a clearly defined 'Englishness' against which other styles could measure themselves.

The process by which tartan cloth and clothing types came together to form 'Highland Dress' was early on described as an 'hallucination'; and the short kilt itself as 'a purely modern costume... bestowed on the Highlanders in order not to preserve their traditional way of life but to ease its transformation; to bring them out of the heather and into the factory.' (H. Trevor Roper, in Hobsbawn and Ranger, 1983, p.22). The allocation of specific tartans to particular clans was mainly effected by Sir Walter Scott and his associates on the occasion of a state visit to Scotland in 1822 - aided by the weaving firm of William Wilson and Son who saw the commercial advantage of building up a stable range of differentiated tartans. A comparable story was enacted in Wales. What followed subsequently was a farrago of fantastically embroidered and sometimes plainly fraudulent 'scholarship', demonstrating the authenticity and antiquity of putative 'traditions'.

There is a cynical and distressing aspect to this story, and to the manner in which highland life was idealised by novelists, painters and the Royal family even while it was being destroyed. Furthermore, the originators and primary clients of these movements were drawn from the very strata of society most active in the incorporation of Scotland and Wales into the hegemony of southern England. The part played by architects and interior designers in creating a setting for this baneful fantasia was repeated, *mutatis mutandis*, all over Europe.

a) Tartan cloth.

The invention of a 'local tradition' is bound up with the development of tourism, with the 'packaging' of local difference and the complicity of the population in turning itself into a spectacle.

b) The Buchanan tartan from *The Clans of the Scottish Highlands,* by R.R. McIan and J. Logan, (1845).

Sample 19

a) St Patricks Church, Jordanstown, by W.H. Lynn, 1867. (Photo; the author).

When we turn to Ireland a different picture emerges, since the construction of difference and 'distinct expression' was bound up with a partly successful political nationalism.

Not only that, there existed real objects and real buildings that could be treated as authentically 'national'. The magnificent decorative art of ancient manuscripts, the metalwork, and the neat and chunky remains of Irish Romanesque buildings were sufficiently distinct from anything else to give the Celtic Revival a basis in fact. Carlyle, visiting the collection of the Royal Irish Academy in 1849 described it as 'a really interesting museum, for everything has a certain authenticity as well as national and other significance, too often wanting in such places.'

b) Detail; a window in the apse. These sharp 'dog-tooth' ornaments are to be found all over Irish Romanesque ornament. Lynn could have studied them directly at, for example, the freshly restored cathedral at Tuam in Co. Galway, or in numerous publications. (Photo; the author).

But a revived nationalism-in-design was not ideologically simple; the main client of the Celtic Revival was the Church of Ireland, and most private patrons belonged to a professional class that was largely Protestant. Thus, when W.H. Lynn designed the beautiful neo-Romanesque Church of St Patrick, at Jordanstown near Belfast in 1867, he was not simply making what he claimed as 'the first attempt in modern times to revive the ancient architecture of Ireland'; he was also involved in an ecclesiological coup to claim the saint for the anglican version of apostolic legitimacy.

But the meanings of motifs are never fixed; like words, they take their significance from the use to which they are put. Once set in motion, the Celtic Revival could hardly fail to take on a 'Fenian' aspect. The interest taken in the Revival by viceregal circles looks, at this distance, like an attempt to defuse its political implications. At the time of writing, the use of Celtic patterns on posters and pamphlets usually signifies in the north a republican rather than nationalist point of origin; the patterns are not used by unionists at all, though the Protestant community was most involved in their retrieval.

Jeanne Sheehy's recent account of the Celtic Revival describes attempts to invent a national costume, and she describes kilts, cloaks, brooches and the use of distinctive green tweed and yellow linen. Architects like Lynn helped to set in motion a considerable and capable craft industry, which produced some outstanding work. But where is it now?

c) Detail of stained glass. Borders such as these are derived not from architecture, but from the manuscripts and metalwork then under close study. Designs from the Book of Kells and the Tara Brooch (discovered in 1850) were printed in *The Grammar of Ornament*. (Photo; the author).

'Anyone who shares the hopes and ambitions of the artists themselves can hardly avoid a sense of disappointment in the fact that a national style failed to materialize clearly. On the other hand, if one stands back from the period and looks at it dispassionately as part of a wider phenomenon, the Irish experience assumes a new dimension. For Ireland was by no means alone. . .' (Sheehy, 1980, p.190).

Something remains of the movement in dance costume. Once a young girl has reached a certain degree of competence she becomes a full member of the troupe, and this moment is marked by her taking up a suitably embroidered costume. These are patterned with the familiar 'Celtic' interlace. Some are elegant, but others are closer to Disneyland than Tara. Nothing so elaborate is required of the boys since in this constellation of ideas, it is the female that is the bearer of 'tradition', i.e. of Nature.

d) Detail of stone-carving. Motifs such as this are now unusable for many people in the North of Ireland, having been appropriated by the 'other sort'. (Photo; the author).

e) Girls in Irish dance costume. (Photo; *The Irish News*).

Sample 20

Amongst Warrington Taylor's list of English attributes, along with 'sweet', 'picturesque', 'homely', 'farmyardish' was 'Japanese'.

This inclusion reminds us how extensively the qualities of Japanese design had impressed themselves upon European taste, not least in Britain. The reasons why this should be so arise from the very preoccupations we have been studying. Japanese designers had no compunction about combining, even within the same item, the pictorial, the emblematic and the abstract aspects of surface pattern. Thus, profound ideological divisions could seem to be bridged at the level of appearances - the new fashion had something for everyone. At the level of symbolism, Japanese motifs and emblems, whilst clearly standing for something, could not be read directly. Thus, the idea of traditional associations could seem to be sustained from an entirely unexpected quarter.

Where furniture was concerned, Japanese woodwork on the small and on the architectural scale seemed to develop further those qualities that had already come to be admired. The 'Queen Anne' revival entailed a revaluing of the lightly constructed elegance of seventeenth- and eighteenth-century carpentery, and the tendency for English furniture to become ever more spare and linear until the new heaviness of the Victorian interior. The tendency toward simplicity and elegance that was already strongly under way, was validated afresh by these discoveries. We can say that japonaiserie did for the Queen Anne revival something that chinoiserie did for the original - it introduced irregular fantasy and lyricism into a plain container, and confirmed an English taste for the picturesque.

a) Wallpaper by E.W. Godwin, 1874; Japanese and Persian motifs. (Coll. Victoria & Albert Museum).

b) Illustration from *The Decoration and Furniture of Town Houses* by Robert Edis, 1881. The Aesthetic Movement by catalogue; spare construction, plenty of space and japonaiserie.

c) Illustration from *The Bedroom and Boudoir* by Lady Barker (1878).

Where craft skill was concerned, what seemed to English designers to be the *ne plus ultra* of Arts and Crafts simplicity and honesty, was seen by the French as an oriental equivalent of the aristocratic

d) Lightshades from Hill House, Helensburgh; designed by C.R. Mackintosh, 1902. Japanese principles of self-evident construction can be found throughout Mackintosh's architecture. (Photo; the author).

Rococco, promoted by aesthete-grandees and poetic warriors. In either case, Japanese design was being appropriated into the value system of another culture and, like the orientalism of an earlier decade, used to spice up the radical uncertainty that was beginning to overcome educated taste.

For the United States, Japanese design could serve as an example of a highly developed elegance that owed nothing to European models; thus it helped to reinforce American cultural nationalism. Arthur Dow's *Composition*, first published in Boston in 1889, uses Japanese illustrations throughout, in an attempt to define the principles of good drawing and composition.

The vogue for Japanese design was promoted through numerous books and articles; but perhaps most importantly through the designs, business activities, travels, books, articles and lectures of the indefatigable Dr Dresser, whose extensive visit to Japan in 1877 is seen in that country as an important moment in cultural history. Dresser was accorded semi-official status, and made a huge collection of items for Louis Tiffany in New York. (See Halen, 1990, ch.2).

The discovery of Japanese design encouraged all those artists and clients everywhere who were looking for definite simplicity and a highly concentrated attention upon a few beautiful objects in each room. This tendency, which was already implied in 'South Kensington' aestheticism, found its complete expression when Japanese elements became as thoroughly integrated as 'Moorish' had been integrated by the 1860s (see sample 22).

e) Illustrations from *Composition* by A.W. Dow. (1913 ed.)

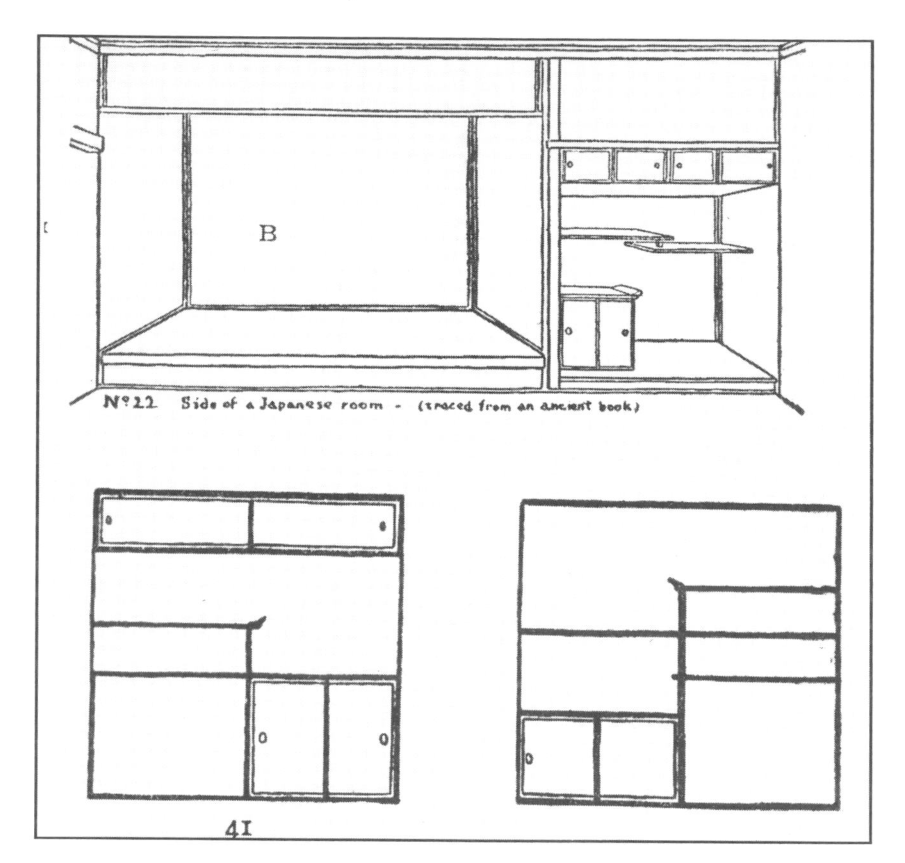

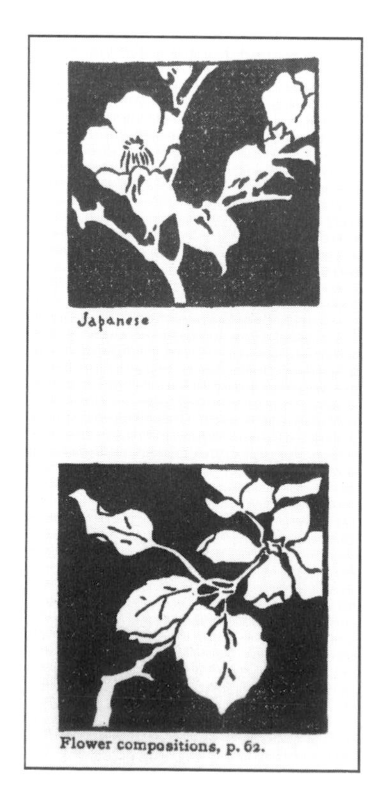

Flower compositions, p. 62.

Massing in two values, from Corot, Daubigny and Hokusai

A COMFORTABLE CORNER.

f) Illustration from *The Drawing Room; its Decoration and Furniture* by Mrs Orrinsmith (1877). Observe the blue and white china, the lightweight furniture, the scroll and the cashmere scarf draped over the stool. Only the statuary seems out of place. Mrs Orrinsmith is against anything she calls 'Victorian' symmetry - 'everything in pairs that can possibly be paired'; the balanced assymetry of this room has its roots in the theory of the picturesque, is being strongly reinforced by a craze for things Japanese, and is looking forward to the next century.

Sample 21

In some of Dresser's later designs, the 'normative' aspect of the discourse begins to reach its culmination. The motif is absorbed into the form of the whole object, so that while it is 'undecorated' - in that it has no applied motifs - it is itself decorative. The object is then seen to be beautiful in the way that objects in nature are beautiful; the connection between beauty and function is 'organic'. The extension of these ideas into architecture, in the early twentieth century, was the work of a 'modern movement' which here is being given an early expression.

An enthusiasm for Venetian and antique glass was common to designers otherwise opposed to one another. Both Dresser and Ruskin met on common ground when they approved the rough finish and molten formations of pre-industrial glassware, and when they despised modern cut glass. Dresser made himself fully acquainted with glass manufacture and working, and produced designs for at least two manufacturers (James Couper and Sons, of Glasgow, and the Tees Bottle Company of Middlesbrough).

Here he has combined industrial bottle-making by moulds with hand-blown craft methods to produce a piece which, whilst making reference to ancient and oriental shapes, is also related to his botani-

a) 'Clutha' Glassware designed by Christopher Dresser and manufactured by James Couper and Sons of Glasgow, 1883. (Coll. Glasgow Museums & Art Galleries).

cal studies. The 'Clutha' range of designs was sold mainly through the firm of Liberty's, and proved very successful. He also had a close business connection with the famous firm of Tiffany in New York whose designs he seems to have influenced. Both the shapes and the subtle colouring are part of that Art Nouveau which marks the end of the European decorative tradition. Each bottle has a stamped signature - could this mean the decorative designer had become the equal of the painter?

He wrote (in 1862) in relation to work in ceramics and glass that 'the endeavour is to produce beauty by the mode of working which is most befitting to the peculiar...material.' This became in the next century the principle of 'truth to material'. In work such as this the symbolic or metaphorical work done earlier by applied motifs has passed over completely into the form of the object. It becomes increasingly difficult to distinguish between the fundamental form of the object, and its decorative aspect. The two appear to be swallowing one another up to produce a new attitude that unites the metaphorical with the functional.

b) 'Clutha' Glassware designed by Christopher Dresser and manufactured by James Couper and Sons of Glasgow, 1883. (Coll. Glasgow Museums & Art Galleries).

Sample 22

a) and b) 'White' furniture, from the apartment of C.R. and M. Mackintosh, 1901. (Coll. Hunterian Art Gallery, Glasgow).

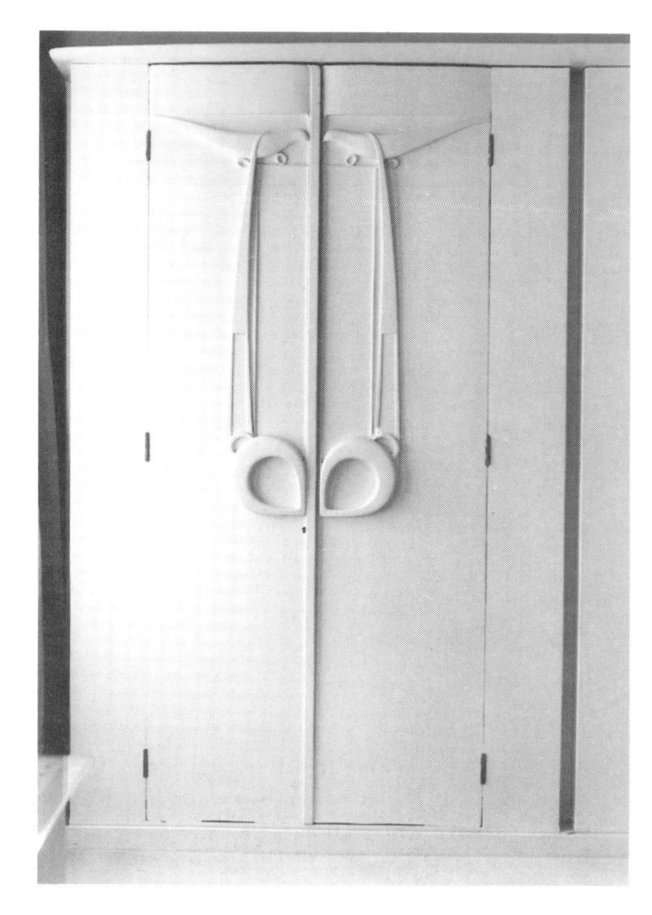

a

The architectural ornament and the decorated interiors created by C.R. Mackintosh represent the furthest point reached by the discourse of decoration in Great Britain. The whole enterprise of his architecture comprises a devotion to the vernacular, a Ruskinian attention to 'natural facts', conventional art-botany, the cult of Japan, abstraction and modernity; his great achievement was to synthesise so many diverse elements into a developing and completely unified style that embraced both the largest and the smallest features of each building he designed.

The 'white rooms' that he created with his wife Margaret Macdonald are of the most extreme refinement. 'Here', wrote a contemporary ' were rooms like dreams'. Surfaces were lacquered to a uniform subtle ivory which disguised all trace of the craftsman's hand; the colours were those of an idealised nudity. These rooms never lose their power to shock nor to induce in the visitor an acute self-consciousness. English designers who might have been expected to be sympathetic greeted the 'Glasgow Style' with terms such as 'unhealthy', 'revolting', 'diseased'; divining, correctly, that this intense and dialectical idealism was in direct opposition to the empirical 'common-sense' and traditionalism of the Arts and Crafts Movement.

However, the main forms of the buildings and their use of materials are all well within the purview of a revived vernacular - a Scottish style that to Mackintosh was the 'pristine' speech of his people, ' as natural as our wild flowers'. The decorative treatment of these exteriors is dramatic,

b

with linear conventions derived from art-botany and a tendency to completely geometrical abstraction.

c) Geometric motif from a writing table in the apartment. (Coll. Hunterian Art Gallery).

This is very well seen in the Scotland Street School, designed in 1904. A great 'Scots thistle as the tree-of-life' motif extends from ground to roofline, three storeys above; leaf or bud motifs in coloured glass set off the starkness of the stair windows, and geometrical reliefs mark out important entrances on the north facade.

Between the most hidden and the most public come spaces such as halls and stairways, which Mackintosh normally filled with a bravura display of carpentry. The

d) Leaf motif in the stairwell, Scotland Street School. (Photo; the author).

e) Detail of relief on the south elevation of Scotland Street School by C.R. Mackintosh, 1904. An appropriately national emblem, in the Pugin manner, setting forth its symbolism directly: the Thistle as the Tree of Life. (Photo; the author).

f) Abstract motifs on the front of Scotland Street School. These squares and triangles are not arbitrary signs; they derive from the treatment of the thistle on the rear of the building. (Photo; the author).

huge 'crossbow' trusses in the Glasgow School of Art (1896-7) are not only decorated by emblems of leaf and heart, but are themselves - like Dresser's glassware - functioning metaphors. The unity of treatment, throughout the building, fuses the decorative with the functional. All parts correlate with one another, as if in imitation of a living creature. But in that case, what has become of decoration as a separate activity?

When we turn to the street outside, and find a version of these trusses holding up the canopy of a contemporary shopping centre, we witness the commodification of a culture - the metaphor is transformed into a signifier of 'Glasgow, City of Culture'.

g) Detail of a shop canopy, Sauchiehall Street, Glasgow, 1989. (Photo; the author).

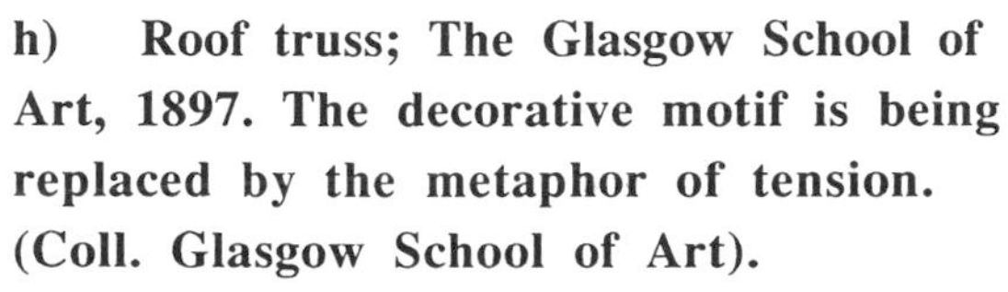

h) Roof truss; The Glasgow School of Art, 1897. The decorative motif is being replaced by the metaphor of tension. (Coll. Glasgow School of Art).

Sample 23

Most decoration has humble intentions; to make a plain place pretty, to mark out a space as your own, to relieve visual boredom. But it still fits within an evolving discourse. This is true even of such minor items as the leaded lights on domestic doors and windows.

The introduction of stained and painted glass into the home was part of the process by which the ecclesiological Gothic Revival passed over into domestic design; it represented, by association, a sanctification of the home as the site of virtue. Early

a

domestic glass took its imagery from Pre-Raphaelite painting, especially the work of Burne-Jones, which provided an iconography that while formally secular, carried with it a claim to spirituality. Among the many studios providing this work, the leading ones were those of Morris and Co. and of Daniel Cottier. By the 1880s, small leaded lights with appropriate scenes or motifs had become a customary feature in every new middle-class house, and each city had its workshops and designers.

b

By 1900, the medium had become one in which Art Nouveau motifs appear, and in which a new imagery of seas and landscapes, of ships and cottages and windmills and sunrises begins to be established.

Belfast is rich in good quality housing from the period of its greatest prosperity, and traces of the Aesthetic Movement and an incipient Art Nouveau are still easy to find. The architect Frederick Tulloch built a small house for himself and included in its details numerous fine touches in glass and metalwork. Whilst some of these can be classed as Art Nouveau, others are closer to work more common in the 1930s. This charming uncertainty of style runs through the entire house. From the perspective of this study, the uncertainty is that of a designer well aware that the continuity of decorative art is under question. He knows what is going on elsewhere, but he does not have the insight to see that Art Nouveau was intended as a total style linked to a renovation of society - a true New Art; so he falls back on a graphic manner which he is probably getting through journals like *The Studio*. He knows something of post-impressionism, perhaps by way of painters like Belfast-born Paul Henry, who had recently returned to Ireland from Paris; but he knows more of the posters of the Beggarstaff Brothers. He has an Arts and Crafts desire for thoroughness of treatment, without the visual grammar to bring about a thorough unity of style.

What to do next? For an architect committed to decorated building, 1905 was a difficult year.

c

d

a),b),c) and d) Stained-glass images set into windows; Frederick Tulloch's house in Belfast, 1905. Little scenes such as this, perhaps deriving from painted tiles, become part of a standardised iconography in the 1920s. (Photos; Barbara Freeman).

e) Window catch from the same house. (Photo; Barbara Freeman).

f) Letter box from the same house. (Photo; Barbara Freeman).

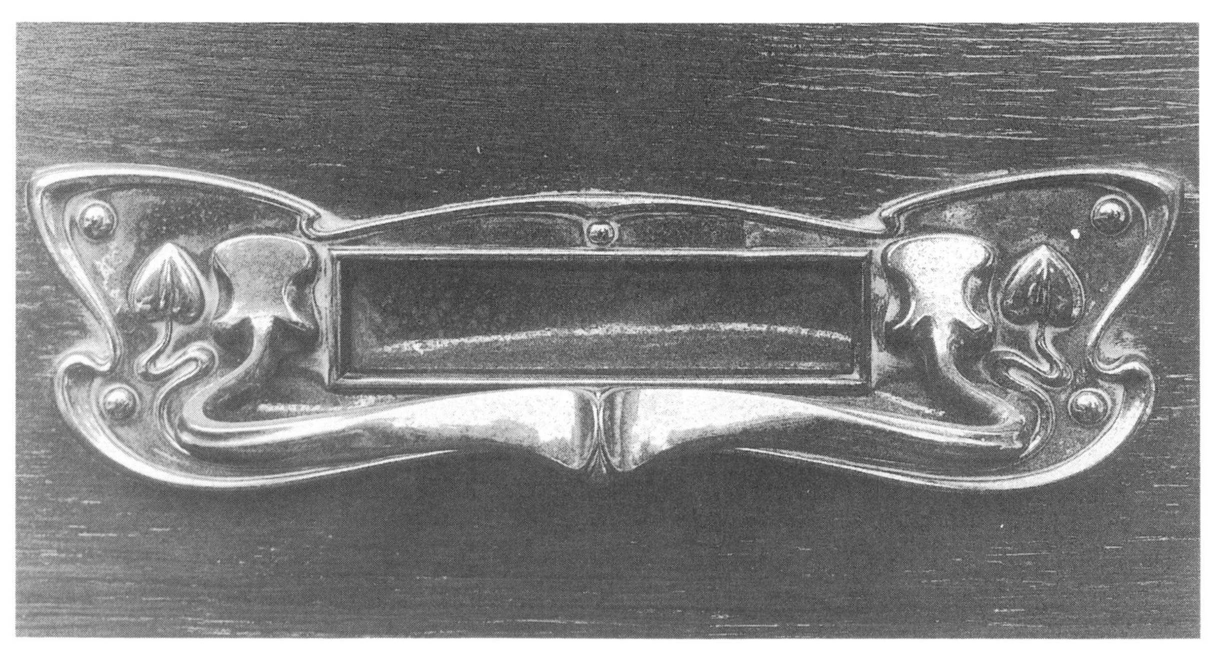

Sample 24

a) Cabinet by Otto Wagner, 1898. (Coll. Victoria & Albert Museum).

The discourse of decoration now reaches a 'critical mass' and, like some stellar phenomenon, collapses inward into self-extinction. Normative theory reaches the point at which it must, logically, deny the validity of the decorative arts that gave it birth.

This is in one sense an historical event; but in another sense it is the logical *denouement* of the increasingly abstract and ambitious character of the conversation. Decoration, of course, continues. Walls are patterned, fabrics are woven and printed, wood is carved and glass blown and metal and clay are wrought into wonderful shapes. But the domain of discourse, in which practice, objects, consumption, ideology and conscious theory meet and reinforce one another, crumbles. Expressed most simply, decoration is no longer taken for granted. And this remains true today.

Adolf Loos' essay of 1908, entitled *Ornament and Crime* takes the example of tattooed flesh with which Owen Jones had initiated the discourse 52 years earlier, and turns the example back on itself. 'The modern man who tattoos himself is either a criminal or a degenerate. . . we have outgrown ornament.' All the nineteenth-century quest for a new style had come to nothing, because style was identified with ornament; 'but therein lies the greatness of our age; that it is incapable of producing a new ornament.' Ornament is 'no longer organically linked with our culture. . . has

b) Chest of Drawers by Adolf Loos, 1899. (Coll. Victoria & Albert Museum).

no connection with the world order.... No ornament can any longer be made by anyone who lives on our cultural level.' (Conrads, 1970 etc).

What Loos and Wagner are doing here, with this domestic furniture - and of course, Wagner is doing it with an eye to prettiness - is to take utilitarian objects such as a cabinet of scientific specimens, a military trunk,and remake them with hairbreadth precision for a fashionable clientele. The same principal could be extended to architectural design. Loos' buildings, spare on the outside, are made opulent within; not by ornament but by superb materials (brass, figured marbles, high quality carpentery etc.).

Le Corbusier (whose education rehearsed the entire discourse beginning with *The Grammar*) transforms Loos' radical passion into an architectural doctrine. The illustrations to *The Decorative Art of Today* (1928) form an ironic counterpart to a text whose intention is to destroy the decorative arts and their exhausted traditions, so that we 'are then obliged to climb by conscious knowledge the long road leading to a new equilibrium.' (See Postscript).

c) Cylinder head; a page from *Aircraft* by Le Corbusier (1935). The fetishisation of machine parts. . . 'The Bohemian poet discovers the machine. . . there he re-encountered, in diabolically perfect and immutable exact form,those functions he had observed in nature.'

d), e) and f) Vignettes from *The Decorative Art of Today* by Le Corbusier (1928).

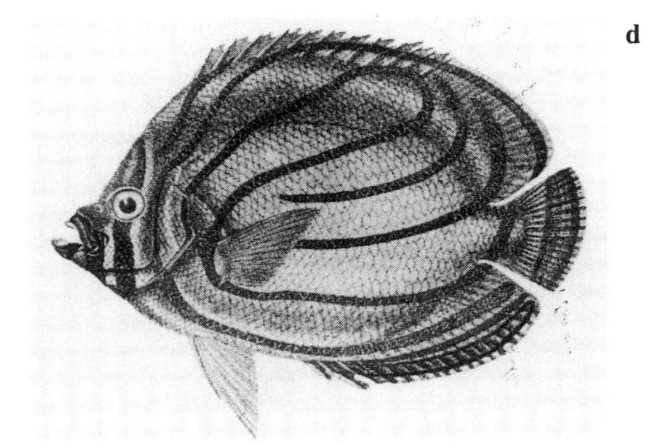

d

d) A sunfish and a section through an electric cable. Typical text illustrations by Lc Corbusier, which present the functional as if it is decorative. Which is which? Now you see it one way, now the other.

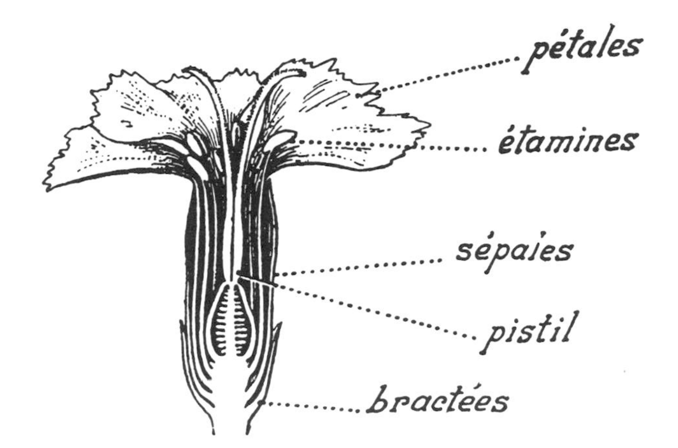

e

e) If natural forms are decorative it is because they exhibit 'The Spirit of Truth'.

f) The decorative art of today? Apeing the past.

f

Sample 25

The attempt to create an entirely undecorated architecture, and to expel the decorative arts from the interior was the last stage of the normative argument, just as the collapse into 'kitsch' or pastiche was the conclusion of its critical alternative. Several examples might given; I have chosen the Wittgenstein house because it stands in relation to the twentieth century much as Jefferson's house at Monticello stands in relation to his epoch. Under its self-effacing appearance it hides an extreme and austere spirit.

The philosopher supervised all details of construction down to the very smallest. 'Pedestrian design problems posed by shelving, closets and other storage space have been solved with the same didactic linearity and with such total absence of miscalculation, such fanatical agreement of proportions, that the house gradually reveals itself as an extravagance beyond Gaudi's wildest hallucinations.' (Indiana, 1985, p.126). There are no ornamental features of any kind whatsoever. The floors are of grey stone and the walls were originally bare plaster; early photographs show unshaded light bulbs and simple but expensive furniture. Windows, doors, radiators and cupboards were all designed by Wittgenstein to the same exacting standards of precision and solidity.

It is easy to see this building as embodying the logical philosophy of *The Tractatus*; easy but deceptive, because behind both house and logic stand prior ethical commitments to a life of authenticity and self-examination. The purpose of philosophy was to rid language and culture of covert metaphysical assumptions, in order to protect and sustain the spiritual and ethical dimensions of life. The values of life cannot be described or expressed; they can only be made manifest. In so far as decoration had come to signify and express the spiritual and the hidden ontological assumptions, Wittgenstein reckoned that, as an attempt to say the unsayable, it had to be foregone. Considered in this light, the absence of ornament can be interpreted as a sort of truth-telling, and its rejection as a gesture of cleansing.

Thus the discourse of decoration comes to a close.

Among the last propositions of *The Tractatus* are the following:

> *'There are no propositions of ethics.*
>
> *It is clear that ethics cannot be put into words.*
>
> *Ethics are transcendental.*
>
> *(Ethics and aesthetics are one and the same.)'*

Such a statement, which may be derived from Ruskin refracted through a reading of Tolstoy, returns the discourse back to its starting point; it should be seen as a working out of ethical problems through an aesthetic medium.

a) House in Vienna designed by Ludwig Wittgenstein, 1923; exterior view S.E elevation. (Photo; Bundesdenkmalamt, Vienna).

b) S.W. elevation. (Photo; Bundesdenkmalamt, Vienna).

Sample 26: Coda and Preamble

The rejection of ornament was not, however, a simple banishment. The unity of decoration and structure and the concept of the artistic interior turns the whole house into a work of art, and allows for an interpenetration of conceptual and professional worlds. This is best illustrated by the De Stijl movement which, using a visual grammar developed through painting, spread a stylistic empire across architecture, furniture, typography and even music.

What we are looking at opposite is an attempt at an English De Stijl - a unity of design process between the fine arts and industrialised building methods. These small houses were the outcome of a collaboration between the builder, Peter Stead, and the sculptor Stephen Gilbert who wrote that 'any attempt to use the artist to make an architectural complex "beautiful" by changing the minor details, balconies, doorways etc. is idiotic, for the artist's obsession today is space-form in a purer sense than that of the architect whose present training makes it hard for him to grasp the essentials of structural space-form in colour.' Both men worked on abstract constructions - 'intermediate objects' - without preliminary drawing. 'As Stephen's became more architectural, mine became more sculptural. I had never found anything more difficult than this - composing directly with colour. But when I got stuck I referred to Mondrian, every time.' They followed strictly, one might say pedantically, the De Stijl principles as laid down by Theo van Doesburg and practised by Gerrit Rietveld. 'Here it is idle to speak of architecture "imitating" painting or sculpture: all concretized in their mode a central principle by which opposing forces could be brought into resolution.' (C. St J. Wilson, 1964).

In time, and designed by Stead alone, a first house was built near Huddersfield, and then a second in collaboration with David Lewis. All parts were industrially prefabricated and quickly assembled on site without difficulty. The frames were of steel and the exterior cladding in colour-anodised aluminium. Interior partitions were in a glass-fibre material using primary colours; the original furnishings were by the Danish designer Poul Kjarholm and, like the house itself, they were assembled from a kit of parts. The houses are known locally as 'them modern things'. In the critical and retrospective atmosphere of English culture, this adventure in normative modernism and 'hi-tech' appears like an oppositional gesture.

Both Stead and Lewis later repudiated their working method, since it had produced a house that was an art-object rather than a designed dwelling; both men have since followed careers in 'participatory' design and the self-build movement.

Stead subsequently built another house, wooden this time, and made from stock size timber by unskilled labour; this is known as 'the Japanese house'.

a) House by Peter Stead, Almondbury, Huddersfield. Anodised aluminium on steel frame, 1959. (Photo; Barbara Freeman).

b) Detail from *The Principles of Neo-Plastic Art* by Theo van Doesburg (1925).

c) House by Peter Stead and David Lewis, 1962. (Photo; Barbara Freeman).

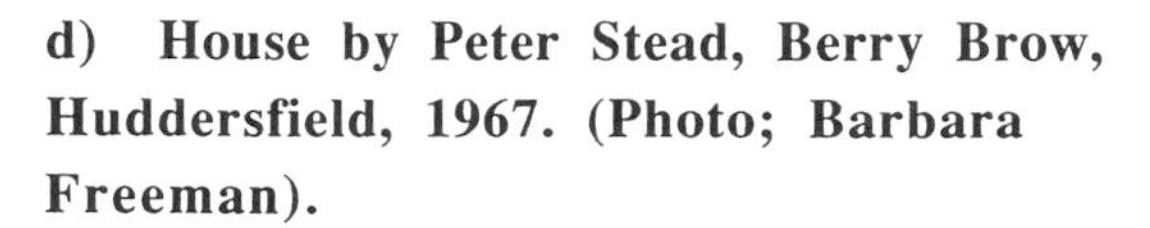

d) House by Peter Stead, Berry Brow, Huddersfield, 1967. (Photo; Barbara Freeman).

What we see in this 'coda' to the discourse is a representation of some of the questions with which we began, not in their original form, but in the form in which they come down to us having passed through one hundred and fifty years. They seem to be the perennial questions of an ever-shifting modernity. What is the relation of decoration to structure? How do the fine and applied arts relate to one another? What are the appropriate materials for today, and what the appropriate design process? What associations attach to what materials and technology? What is the meaning of pattern or its absence? That the original discourse came to an end, did not resolve those problems.

To investigate them further will require a Postscript.

—Postscript—

'Our discourse always tends to slip away from our data towards the structures of consciousness with which we are trying to grasp them; or, what amounts to the same thing, the data always resist the coherency of the image which we are trying to fashion of them.' Hayden White[1]

I began this book by describing it as 'developing an intellectual narrative' - a discourse powered by antithetical tendencies that worked either with or against the grain of industrial modernisation. I described the study of decoration as 'part of the study of the many ways in which modern society searches for its meanings.' An intellectual history, however, like any other, runs the risk of absolutising its own methods into a system of total explanation and the impulse toward an easy symmetry needs to be resisted. I am aware that in my desire to construct an explanatory scheme I have (in the dialectic of normative and critical movements) created a mythic apparatus, the sort of intellectual engine that may be a good servant but is certainly a bad master.

This is especially the case when we come closer to our own experience; we are not neutral, and any conclusions we may reach have always some prescription implied in them. Thus to look back again at the origins of the nineteenth-century discourse of decoration is also at the next step to anticipate possible futures.

* * * *

We should regard the discourse of decoration as a polemical arena which enabled certain positions and beliefs to be made clearer. It came into being because the relations between art and industry, between art and design, between craft and industry and between other more or less antithetical concepts needed clarification.[2] These relations touched upon many matters; begining with the self-definition of a new profession, that of the 'designer' or 'industrial artist', the scope of the discourse constantly enlarged to include everything comprised under the heading of modernity. In more general social terms, the domestic interior had become the site on which 'particularist' differences could be asserted and social identities made manifest.

It is customary to date its formal inception from the calling of the Parliamentary Commission into Arts and Manufactures in 1835. This inquiry resulted in a mass of evidence from designers, manufacturers and teachers which, taken together, give a remarkable picture of the state of debate at that time. But it shows us that the discourse was already well under way. There was a large and growing literature addressed to the topic, in the papers of architectural associations, trade journals, archaeological societies and in writings such as those of D.R. Hay and George Phillips. Though these writings had diverse aims, all were in some measure concerned with the problems of contemporary practice.

The ostensible purpose of the Parliamentary Commission was to enquire into the quality of British manufactures and the possibility of their improvement; it was the brainchild of the 'Philosophical Radicals' in Parliament. This energetic faction sought to exploit the balance between Whigs and Tories to the advantage of a scientific and capitalist programme of modernisation. Its philosophical basis was primarily utilitarian, and it included close followers of Jeremy Bentham and J.S. Mill in its most active membership. (William Ewing who chaired the commission with acute partiality, Charles Thompson who set it up, and John Bowring who was its most regular member and occasional chairman, were all 'Radicals'. Bowring was Bentham's executor and the editor of the Radical journal *The Westminster Review.*)[3] Their strictly political purpose in calling the Inquiry was to ally the Radical faction with industry and 'the manufacturing population' against the Royal Academy, to them the centre-piece of inherited privilege and aristocratic cultural values; and thus to help in a realignment of public opinion. Much of the evidence given to the inquiry indicates the assault was sustained and planned, with frequent complaints about the Academy's 'exclusive and oligarchical character'. The report that followed the inquiry alleged, naturally enough, that academies 'narrow the proper basis of all intellectual excellence - mental freedom'.[4] The subsequent development of the discourse, even its conclusions, follow from these aggressive premises though it is doubtful if the protagonists fully understood the consequences in terms of design and its theory.

In design theoretical terms the Radical project implied the overthrow of the academical pyramid of status which placed 'the higher arts' of architecture, painting and sculpture at the top, and the lowly pattern-drawer at the bottom; with an assumed entailment of quality from the top down. Joshua Reynolds' founding 'Discourse' to the Academy lays out this dogma absolutely plainly. 'No taste can be formed in manufactures; but if the higher Arts of Design flourish, these inferior ends will be answered of course.' The incompatibility of Benthamite utilitarianism and its continental cousin, positivism, with the cultural traditions of the Academy was, at the time, more guessed at than fully understood: both the evidence and the report bear witness to a considerable intellectual confusion in which ideological sleight-of-mind and honest effort are inextricably mixed. It took a full forty years before Christopher Dresser could draw the logical inference; that decoration, 'being wholly of mental origin', was in principal superior to pictorial art; thus was the intellectual structure of the academies dismantled and the aim of the Radicals realised.

Within the philosophical terms of the discourse, this was the proper and logical conclusion to be drawn; but in ideological terms it represents the victory of one set of social and philosophical attitudes over another. In Gramscian terms, it represents the hegemony of one social formation over another; considered in this way, the discourse (in all its twistings and turnings) enacted the struggle for mastery within different factions of the ruling class, each seeking its own version of modernity.

Initiated by utilitarians, the discourse provoked an opposite and equal reaction. John Ruskin described himself as simultaneously a 'communist' and a 'Tory of the old school'; that he could do so and that his attitudes should find such a ready response indicates how much of human experience and culture the Benthamism of the Radicals neglected. Ruskin's perfectly articulated loathing of the 'steam' philosophy sought to maintain a version of academic teaching - quality still flowed down to decorative design from the heights above, but it did so on terms that were in principal anti-academic and ahistorical. As we have seen, the differences between the two camps is made especially clear by considering the attitudes taken toward drawing in the process of design. But these in turn imply different concepts of culture. Ruskin affirms culture as 'local association and historical memory', but does so on ontological foundations ('Nature') that generalise real cultural and historical differences and push authentic experience back toward the 'natural' condition of the vernacular. Normative pedagogy, on the other hand, sought to be acultural and abrogate to itself the character of a science. By asserting that there were 'laws' of ornament it claimed to stand prior to any actually existing culture. Such a claim, of course, is a form of intellectual imperialism, though we should resist the easy temptation to reduce it merely to that level, since (as we shall see), it has entailments much wider and more general than political empire.

It would have been simple to set out these alternative traditions in terms of binary opposition - of romantic versus rationalist, abstraction versus empathy, or idealist versus empiricist. But a closer attention to the movements of thought and practice, both considered in themselves as attitudes and tactics, and historically as evolving complexes of reality, shows that we have to do with reciprocal action in a dialectic of continuous modification. Nor should we seek to fix individuals in their working lives too firmly within either camp. The thoughtful critic and the busy professional designer, as much as the enthusiastic follower of fashion, could and often did embody the shifting tensions of the discourse and, thus, lived out a contradiction. The normative and the critical are not fixed positions, but mobile and responsive energies.

Both, moreover, had essential features in common. The 'South Kensington school' was openly ahistoric; if the *a priori* conditions for good ornament are the same for all epochs and cultures, teaching need not claim historical justification nor transmit any particular historical culture. The aim was, in essence, to supercede the past - indeed, the aim in some circles was an Hegelian culmination of history which had little foundation in positivism. But the Ruskinian appeal to 'Nature' and to the 'natural facts' of vision also cuts through any attempt at an academic or historicist teaching in favour of a direct 'infantine' apprehension of reality. It claimed to be neither new nor old, but timeless, being based upon an essence called 'Truth'. This, as Ernst Gombrich observes, was the time bomb under the foundations of the academic hierarchy, which in other respects Ruskin professed to support.[5] But above all, both are profoundly concerned to raise the level of debate about design, decoration and 'art industry'; and in so doing to raise the status of the 'ornamentist' by taking decoration with extreme seriousness. This should not surprise us at all, since the social and economic importance of design and manufacture, both as a signifying system and as a generator of investment capital, was immense. The servicing of the modern domestic interior has been an essential feature of modern economic life. The ideological rationale for this is further brought out by Wornum's distinction between 'symbolic' and 'aesthetic' modes of decoration. This is, as already observed, a Kantian distinction. By appropriating decoration into the realm of disinterested aesthetic pleasure, independent of the good or the useful, Wornum effects the equation between the decorative and the fine or 'higher' arts toward which the discourse in its normative aspect was always aiming. Hereby the new profession of 'designer' begins to acquire the intellectual dignity it had not hitherto possessed, and discussion about ornament can take on a new seriousness.[6] This collective professional enterprise much resembles the successful attempt made during the Renaissance to give painting the status of a liberal art. Amongst other things that we are witnessing here is the cultural solidification of a trade inseparable from industrial society, and the philosophical validation of an activity on which industry depends.

What further follows from this is the downgrading of popular 'symbolic' taste, as demonstrated in *Hard Times* (quoted above; sample 2).

Whereas Ruskin's support for naturalistic drawing and 'natural facts' as the basis of good decoration was an appeal for cultural continuity, Sissy Jupe's insistence on 'fancy' signifies that the disruption of the continuum of decorative style had already taken place. Let us not be mistaken in this; Wornum's two modes are intimately related to a separation of the classes. I can't do better here than quote from the work of Pierre Bourdieu:'By contrast, working class people, who expect every image to fulfil a function, if only that of a sign, refer, often explicitly, to norms of morality or agreeableness in all their judgements. . . popular naturalism recognizes beauty in the image of a beautiful thing. . . . Nothing is more alien to popular consciousness than the idea of an aesthetic pleasure that, to put it in Kantian terms, is independent of the charming of the senses.' To continue, 'aesthetic stances in matters like. . . home decoration are opportunities to experience or assert one's position in social space, as a rank to be upheld or a distance to be kept. . . . (however). strategies aimed at transforming the basic dispositions of a life style into a system of aesthetic principles. . . are, in fact, reserved for members of the dominant class.' [7] Ruskin, as a 'Tory of the old school', is attempting to validate the basic dispositions by entering into a debate that will align popular naturalism with high intellectual culture 'of the old school', and bring into being a counter-alliance against the Radicals.

We can now see that Dickens' lampoon of South Kensington dogma is deadly accurate; it represents the irreconcilable difference between the modernisers and those who are modernised. We note also that he could see no feasible alliance; between fact and fancy there was no middle ground to occupy. The little episode depicted in *Hard Times* is one of the primal scenes of modern taste and its consequences are with us to this very day.

In stressing the ideological character of the discourse, it is not my intention to reduce ornament to the mere illustration of social status. It is clear that we have to do with a classical problem of 'base-superstructure' relations. The view taken here is that the origins and growth of the discourse cannot be understood without recourse to an analysis of the class and social-formation interests of the professional groups that set it in motion. Nor can it be separated from more narrowly technical and productive considerations (the demand for conventional linear drawing, for example, is certainly connected to the constraints of designing for machine production, automatic routing, pattern-moulding etc.). This technical aspect was well recognised at the time. But once a discourse of this kind is moving forward, it has the autonomy of any other intellectual engine; the tendency will always be for the conclusions to follow from the premises rather than from the understood assumptions and perceived goals of its initiators. The 'Philosophical Radicals' did not expect the extension of their power to entail the extinction of their ornament.

Moreover, the desire for decoration appears to be a human constant, deeply related to perceptual processes and to the principles of pleasure. Thus, while any specific use of decoration may be interpreted 'ideologically' as part of a signifying system, decoration *per se* cannot be so reduced.

* * * *

The motives of the Parliamentary Committee of Inquiry were frankly political and utilitarian in the narrowest sense; there is some distance to be traversed between that position and the dionysiac enthusiasm of a Louis Sullivan, and thence to the final rejection of ornament and the downgrading of all the decorative arts. It is necessary to look at this ground once again, because it is the site on which a modern sensibility was built, in all its splendours and disasters. It will, of course, be understood that I am concerned primarily with British sources; though a similar trajectory was followed in continental Europe. The following summary of the normative branch of our topic repeats points made above, but leads toward a speculative conclusion.

The discourse has two origins; the first is internal to architectural debate, being concerned with the right relation between decoration and structure (exemplified by Pugin's writings), and between colour and the function of the wall (Owen Jones, Gottfried Semper, Hittorff and others). The second is utilitarian in both the narrow and the philosophic sense, concerned with the training, status and methods appropriate for the burgeoning 'art industries'. The pressure for adequate training required a theory of decoration.

The creation of a theory of decoration required more than historical scholarship and the demands of utility; it meant the construction or adaptation of a world-picture of some form. The influence of Saint-Simonist ideas, and of Comtean positivism, runs all through the language of the discourse during the 1840s. The trinity of 'science, industry and art' which the new theory hoped to unite in an educational programme, springs directly from these sources. The great monument of this stage is *The Grammar of Ornament*, whose central assumption is that evidence adduced from culture is as universal and timeless as evidence from nature; and that, therefore, decoration can be described by laws equivalent to the laws of science. More particularly, that the process of abstraction and generalisation characteristic of the South Kensington drawing curriculum was validated by universalised culture and was therefore 'natural'. Such a theory is, in truth, far from positivistic; it is permeated throughout with a sort of utopian longing. One writer has observed shrewdly that 'It is a theory in waiting, tuned in readiness to some unlikely broad and deep social change it cannot even define, much less bring about, but upon which the true completion of its project would ultimately depend.'[8] That social change, for Jones, was the realisation of the unity of mankind through science, industry and art; the Saint-Simonist parousia. At this point the ground of the theory ceases to be 'scientific' or 'positive' and develops its own form of idealism. This covert idealism surfaced finally in the writings of Le Corbusier, in a distinct and radical form.

The development of 'art-botany' represented a further stage, since it detached the creation of the decorative motif from historical culture and attempted to ground it in the new vision of nature as hidden structure. Thus theories of expression could no longer rely on associationist ideas, upon 'local association' and 'historical memory', but had to begin to seek other types of analogical validation (musical, biological etc.). Following the botanical model, the distinction between decoration and structure, which was central to architectural theory, was elided in favour of an 'organic' unity of artistic effect. Throughout the later part of the century, the normative discourse made ever more frequent use of evolutionary and organic analogies to explain this process. In the course of these analogies the crucial distinction between a random, materialist evolution (as proposed by Darwin) and a teleological, goal-directed evolution was overlooked. This should be interpreted as the return of a repressed 'natural theology' back into the culture as a whole and into design theory specifically. (Dresser and Mackmurdo).

The penultimate stage was reached when decoration was no longer given meaning by historical culture but by 'absolutist' constants of expression or by radical novelty, and was progressively integrated into architecture. This highly abstract conception of design was increasingly justified by transcendental arguments, which strove to combine evolutionary, spiritual and economic premises by recourse to a 'higher synthesis'. The same phenomena can be observed in the fine arts. This represented in the realm of design the much wider rejection of positivism that took place throughout Euro-American culture in the last years of the nineteenth century. In the British context this is most clearly observed in the birth, flowering and death of the 'Glasgow Style'.[9] In the United States it is best represented by the work and writings of Sullivan.[10]

Thus we arrive at a situation in which the relations between the fine or 'higher' arts and the lowly decorative arts have been completely redefined, to the degree that in the unity of the artistic interior the previous systematic distinctions have entirely disappeared. This is perhaps as much an apotheosis of decoration, as its rejection. This stage is best represented by movements such as 'De Stijl' and aspects of Russian constructivism and considered in anthropological terms it marks the end of the European decorative traditions. Considered in ideological terms this culmination of the discourse represents the achieved hegemony of industrial modernity and the social groups that set it in motion.

Nineteenth-century writers on decoration were especially keen to ascribe decorative styles and their motifs to specific cultures[11]; this was a result of their taxonomic approach and would also seem to spring from the contemporary studies of 'folk' and 'national' styles in music, and comparative linguistics. If patterns and motifs in music and language could be given national or ethnic labels, why not patterns and motifs in decoration? And consequently, if cultures and peoples could be defined by the decoration they use, what does one make of a culture that has no, or no consistent, ornament?

This book has been based on the assumption that the desire for decoration is one of the constants of culture; that it is one of the permanent constituents of human life. The grounds for this assumption must now be made clear, at least in outline, if we are to consider a culture without decoration.

The desire for decoration appears to have two main foundations, the first of which is perceptual and biological in origin. Studies of perception and the processes of vision demonstrate clearly that sight is not merely receptive, but active. The optical system hunts for shapes, figures and irregularities. When it is deprived of them by completely blank surfaces the continuous activity within the eye-brain system creates the appearance of disturbances upon the blank wall. The ability to recognise figure-ground relationships is an essential feature of the system, and almost certainly related to biological needs whose origins lie far back within the prehistorical experiences of the human species. I say almost certainly, because this is not a matter that can be fully demonstrated; it is, however, the most reasonable inference. Within the natural environment, the ability to distinguish between figure and ground is essential for life; within the artificial environment, figure and ground relations (typically, motifs upon a wall) serve to relieve the tension of the continuously 'hunting' eye-brain system. This relief of tension is pleasureable. This pleasure in turn is related to other pleasures, psychic in character, whose origins lie in earliest experience. The slow emergence of the figure out of the ground re-enacts the earliest moments of recognition - of our mother's face, for example, or of any other loved object. The alternation of rough and smooth, so important in the pleasures of architecture, touch upon even earlier feelings; rhythms, repetitions, and subtle variations all induce pleasure and a pleasureable anxiety. It seems also to be important for the life of the imagination that we can at will dissolve the distinctions between figure and ground, take in total and enveloping effects, and return to undifferentiated vision by intent. There is a considerable literature to this effect, and numerous controversies, which it is not necessary to investigate here.[12]

These foundations, which are both essential to the species and an integral stage in the formation of each individual, are then elaborated and codified by culture - that is, through manufacture, symbolisation, cooperative relations of many kinds. The stages through which the primary demands for security, pleasure and signification pass before taking on concrete shape as the decorative arts are of enormous complexity, but appear to be common to all human societies. At least, we can be confident that no society is known to us without some form of ornament. If we can, for a while, free ourselves of the strait-jacket of taste, it is possible to glimpse the outlines of a materialist theory that would relate decoration to the biological bases of life. Such a theory would tell us very little about any real decorative style, but it would give us a starting point to investigate the attempt at a systematic rejection of ornament.

The objection made to much twentieth-century design, that it is 'inhuman', is related to this; when confronted by perfectly smooth or uniform surfaces we nearly always feel nervous and disatisfied. This is especially the case on a large scale; the eye hunts for irregularity with increasing frustration. Perfectly smooth large walls are felt to be oppressive, unless their proportions are perfect. (I hope I can leave aside a discussion on what 'perfect proportion' means here, except to remark that there is some as yet undetermined relation between size and proportions and quality of surface that is as basic as the figure-ground relation.) That this is a truism of popular taste does not invalidate its central meaning.

A very large blank brick wall is more endurable than one of sheet steel, because every brick is an individual. For example, sitting at this desk I can look up through my window and see nothing but such a wall; through 'idle' (actually, busy) contemplation, I have come to recognise patterns and 'figures' in this wall and I no longer regard it as 'oppressive', but as a sort of game or playing field. This pleasure is not specifically to do with the associations of the material, brick, which has certain pleasureable connotations, because a rusted and weathered steel wall might offer similar opportunities for play. Design, especially interior design, that neglects or deliberately ignores these ludic pleasures, is nearly always an impoverished and impoverishing design. An extreme austerity is endurable only when it serves some particular accepted purpose - as in the laboratory or the convent. The same principles appear to be true in smaller objects, though of course these cannot 'oppress' us because they do not enclose. At least we can be confident that some form of decorative treatment is the norm except in special and well-recognised cases.

Loos' claim that modern man has outgrown the decorative arts was echoed and amplified in Le Corbusier's book *The Decorative Art of Today* which was first published in 1925. The main premise of the book is that 'Decorative art can no longer exist, any more than can the "styles" themselves. . . decorative art can no longer be considered compatible with the framework of contemporary thought.' This is because 'The machine. . . is bringing about a reformation of the spirit across the world. . . (it) is conceived within the spiritual framework which man has constructed for himself and not in the realm of fantasy...the lesson of the machine lies in the pure relationship of cause and effect.'[13] The book as a whole is a rich and polemical commentary on the huge Expositions des Arts Decoratifs which occurred in Paris in the year of publication; his special objection is to the various attempts to resuscitate decoration after Loos had declared it dead.

The section that concerns us most is the final section, entitled 'Confession'. This a polemic and humourous account of his education from a start in the decorative arts to its conclusion in the new undecorated architecture. 'My master had said: "Only nature can give us inspiration, can be true, can provide a basis for the work of mankind. But don't treat nature like the landscapists who show us only its appearance. Study its causes, forms and vital development, and synthesize them in the creation of ornaments." He had an exalted conception of ornament, which he saw as a kind of microcosm.'[14] Then, after much practical learning and study in museums, he visits Germany and acquaints himself with modern engineering at the service of design. He witnesses an engine whose function is to give machine-forged iron the appearance of rough hand-forging. 'What an atrocity! . . . fifteen years later I am of the clear opinion that industry by itself is following the course of its own evolution; the designer-decorator is the enemy, the parasite, the false brother.' The question is really 'Can decorative artists with sketches made on paper at the call of fancy, modify the inexorable, almost automatic exigencies of industrial technology.' He becomes convinced that 'the achievements of the past were complete, and that a continuous and irreversible forward movement grips one epoch after another, and in due course leads the peoples of the world on to the next stage. . . one conviction: we must begin again from scratch.'

With the benefit of hindsight, what we see as most striking in *The Decorative Art of Today* (and many other similar writings could be cited to the same effect),is the assumption that in 1925 technological evolution is 'inexorable, almost automatic'. From the point of view of the discourse, this is the place from which we set out - the Saint-Simonist infatuation with 'science, industry and art', now infused with evolutionary assumptions. With the all-important difference, that the machine has made the realisation of this dream possible; it is occurring NOW. Right before our eyes!

In Le Corbusier's writings, the progressively growing idealism of the discourse takes on its final metaphysical form - it justifies contemporary science and industry as products of natural evolution and sets them forth as the only true source of art. This is natural theology without the divinity. It effects a world-renovation in which it is imperative to 'start from scratch'. The rejection of ornament is not just a rejection of history, 'styles' and social 'decorum'. It is a challenge, at the deepest level, to human identity. It announces a new epoch which will require a 'new man'.

There are points of comparison here, too extensive to investigate now, with the rejection of sacred imagery at the Reformation. The pictures of saints, virgins and miracles that were 'executed' by the civil and religious authorities during the sixteenth century were destroyed not just because they had no justification in scripture, but because they were the external manifestation of the internal psychic imagery which had to be obliterated before the cultural revolution could be effected.[15] Churches were symbolically cleansed with whitewash after images were removed: and this, notoriously, is what Le Corbusier himself proposes. 'Every citizen is required to replace his hangings, his damasks, his wallpapers, his stencils with a plain coat of white ripolin. His home is made clean...Everything is shown as it is. Then comes inner cleanliness ... with ripolin you will throw away what has served its purpose and is now scrap.'[16] For the architect, this symbolic cleansing was also a return to origins - a fundamentalism. 'Peoples are then obliged to climb by conscious knowledge the long road leading to a new equilibrium.'

The Decorative Art of Today is a sarcastic, often very funny, book; but its guiding images are deadly serious, and their tone and conclusions were paralleled in numerous other publications and manifestos across Europe. The growth of the 'International Style' in architecture, the 'modernist' interior, the more general depletion of traditional ornament are today, in some quarters, seen as an aberration. But a study of the discourse suggests that they are the central cultural statement of the industrial epoch towards which or from which everything else is to be related. And every people, nation or culture that is touched by industrialisation must go through a similar narrow gate.

* * * *

The discourse of decoration led to its denial; but that did not mean decoration ceased to exist. Floral wallpapers, patterned fabrics, moulded ceilings and fancy goods of every description continued to be made; and new objects, needs and materials offered themselves for inventive treatment. The demand for decoration, having such profound roots in human life and in economic activity, could not be stemmed by mere argument. But serious-minded architects and designers in many fields attempted to divest their practice of overtly decorative elements and increasingly treated the arts of ornamentation as, at best, trivial. Such attitudes and arguments continue to influence our environment today. Furthermore, the denial also meant that what further development of decorative art did take place was inspired by other sources, not from within its own entrails. The attrition of traditional ornament and the ever higher demands made of decoration, by leading toward abstraction, created a void that was filled with new decorative ideas deriving directly from painting and sculpture and, to a lesser degree, from machine production and the new architecture. The continuity of decorative art was broken irreparably.

A very good case can be made to show that during the latter half of the nineteenth century, the discourse of decoration continually fed the parallel activity of painting; that it provided paradigms and models (of 'flatness', of figure-ground relations, of quasi-musical coloration) from which painters learned much. But at some point in the early years of this century this flow of ideas and inspiration was reversed. Movements in painting such as post-impressionism and, later, Fauvism lent themselves to decorative extrapolation because they had taken on something of the decorative from the very beginning. This can be seen clearly in the work of Henri Matisse, which has proved such a fertile source of ideas for fabric designers in the past fifty years. Likewise, the visual vocabulary of cubism proved very amenable both to surface pattern and three-dimensional work; not, we should add, the insurgent experimental cubism of Braque and Picasso, but the academic and domesticated cubism of their followers. The design of Sonia Delaunay is an especially vivid exemplar of the penetration of fashion and interior design by painterly concerns. In Britain, the Omega Workshop and the vorticists were also early examples of this 'reversal'.

In a more radical departure, the De Stijl programme, originating within the concerns of painting, deliberately set out to resystematise all forms of design according to its own principles. (See sample 25 above). Most radical of all were the several strands of the Russian avant-garde, which proposed a 'materialised utopia' in which the distinctions between art, design, architecture and decoration were all subsumed under the concept of 'production'. Important too are the 'calls to order' that reoccur in different disguises during the interwar years and since, which have reasserted figuration in painting and various forms of neo-classicism in architecture. These threw decoration back on its own depleted resources, resulting in a heavy, opulent 'monumental style'.

Architectural writers such as Banham and Collins have described these phenomena in terms of the 'influence' of industrial design and painting on architecture. I believe it is nearer the case to describe the relations between painting, decoration and architecture as being those of 'interpenetration'. This was not only at the level of ideas, but in professional demarcations; these are best summed up by the career of Gerrit Rietveld who, as a cabinet-maker inspired by painting, became a founder-member of the International Congresss of Modern Architecture (CIAM)[17]. Or by that of Peter Behrens who began as a painter, turned craftsman, and transformed himself steadily into both architect and complete industrial designer. The new non-representational painting which did so much (according to Collins) to form thinking about interior design and the relations between plane, space and mass, was a painting whose leading concepts owed much to 'decorative' ideas. The 'organic' analogy, which had an independent existence within architectural thinking, was refined and strengthened by decorative 'art-botany' which, by eliding the distinction between structure and ornament, prepared the way for the formal rejection of decoration. . . etc. This is a complicated story which we are far from understanding. The aim of this study has been to stress the role played by decorative ideas and to suggest that in some cases the discourse of decoration had priority over the others. But by the 1920s the flow of ideas outward from the sphere of decoration had ceased.

In terms of cultural hierarchy, this 'reversal' represents a sort of renewed academicism, in which the old 'higher arts of design' are once again at the top of the pyramid and quality flows down from the fine arts into manufacturing. The resultant styles (and I am thinking here particularly of the inter-war years) are often beautiful and interesting, and they fully deserve investigation; but to tell their story would require a change in conceptual framework and intellectual method. This would require another volume, very different in character. Yet the force of this 'reversal' needs to be investigated because it is the negative outcome of the discourse we have been studying, and because we continue to live with its results.

I put forward the following argument more as hypothesis than conclusion: my concern has always been to focus upon certain sorts of question rather than to provide secure answers. I believe that as a generalised hypothesis it will hold good, but that (as in any such account) a study of detail will raise endless contrary possibilities.

The denial of ornament was the logical conclusion of the normative drive of the discourse; it represented in ideological terms the coming-to-dominance of its client's social formations. (In this respect, the Art Nouveau of the crucial period stands as a sign of the increasing confidence and self-consciousness of the new elite on the verge of its success.) This denial has two aspects, which interplay with one another but which cannot be reduced to either. On the one hand it announces the victory of the scientistic and anti-metaphorical radicals who initiated the discourse; transposed into the production terms of 1920 this meant the emergence of rationalised and monopolised industry from its origins in early and individual capitalism. (This is most clearly expressed in the polemics and professional adventures of Le Corbusier.) From this followed the idea of an 'International Style', of international standardisation and at length that tendency to global uniformity which makes every city centre much like every other.

On the other hand, the increased abstraction of decoration represented the positivist's crisis of meaning, which compelled him toward a transcendent resolution. Thus the 'pure' forms of the new buildings could work directly upon our souls because their forms were the 'constants' of expression, (Le Corbusier).[18] Thus, it would be possible to create a universal culture by holding to 'universal' means of expression, resulting in an environment 'pure and complete in its beauty' (Mondrian).[19] Thus forms 'of mental origin' announce 'the early morning of this long-hoped-for day' (Dresser). That is to say that the denial of ornament contains both utopianism and instrumentality.[20]

It is just this combination that critics of 'modernism' find most objectionable. The main difficulty in blending the utopian with the instrumental is that it requires a religious dedication more in the province of monks than of everyday lives. The main difficulty in having it accepted is that an undecorated and universal style supposes unanimity and does not afford the chance of social differentiation. It blocks off access to difference both at the level of individual whim (which, being rooted in the pleasure principle, is no trivial matter), and it does so at the social level by assuming a unity of interest and taste between different social formations, and classes, and nations. Being egalitarian, it makes impossible that stimulation of novelty, fantasy and spurious individuality without which consumer-led capitalism withers. The 'particularist' set of shifting norms, described by Agnes Heller as the means by which social identity is created under modern conditions, becomes impossible.

Thus, it becomes necessary polemically to reduce what was held to be the end of the 'styles', to just another historical style, and an aberrant one at that. This is nothing whatever to do with a supposed 'pluralism' or the supposed decay of any 'master narrative', and much more to do with the promotion of high consumption, a rapid turnover of styles and the maintenance of social difference.

It is here that the role of the avant-garde fine arts in the creation of new decorative styles became possible - indeed, essential. The avant-garde, though it may appear in the mask of a bohemian opposition, was always directed from the main body; it was a necessary element in the modernisation we have been studying. This was always recognised in the decorative field, through governmental support and institutions. But the official recognition of the new fine arts begins with the development of alternative academies and schools, with the growth of collections of modern art, and with new state institutions patronising new art. From around 1920 onward the avant-garde became part of the institutions of the state and the public authorities. One could cite such examples as the founding of the Bauhaus, the employment of Robert Delaunay in the 1925 Exposition, the recognition accorded to Monet by the French state and the incorporation of Italian futurism into Italian fascism. This process was notably late in Britain.

The result, through the mechanism of state and corporate patronage, was a flow of new decorative arts, succeeding one another with rapidity and subsequently appearing 'dated' because they occurred in no dialectical order. Once the nineteenth-century discourse was dissolved there was no necessary relation between one taste and another; all is swallowed up in consumption. One is left, today, with a plurality of items from which, by selection, ephemeral 'norms' in the form of fashions can be constructed.

At the risk of overboldness we can assert that, through the nineteenth century, changes in decorative taste related logically to the previous taste; but that with the break in continuity, changes now related to other orders of influence and logical priority. Decoration ceased to maintain the consistency and autonomy that it had earned in the previous hundred years. This autonomy had not been in any sense absolute as changes in taste were always linked to the self-definition of social groups; but the modes in which these changes were precisely realised, through the choice of motifs, materials, methods of production etc. followed lines of development that already inhered in the discourse. As the discourse collapsed, different decorative styles coexisted or succeeded one another without logical connection. And this remains the case down to the present day.

It is therefore necessary to bring this book to its conclusion. I had imagined, at the start, continuing in the same manner and foresaw myself writing further short passages on selected topics - the fetishisation of machine form, the painter as decorator etc.. But, as I have argued, these would have to belong to another order of explanation and a different intellectual narrative. Indeed, it might be necessary to drop the idea of a 'story' altogether and to consider the nature of recent and contemporary decoration in the 'vertical' rather than 'horizontal' dimension. The problem here is similar to that distinction made by linguists between the 'synchronous' state of the language at any one time (a vertical section across the flow of development), and the transverse or 'diachronous' cut along the flow. I am suggesting that the continuity of the discourse enables us to make an historical 'diachronic' sense of nineteenth-century decoration that cannot be brought forward into present times, which can only be given sense 'synchronically'. This is another way of saying that contemporary experience resists historical explanation.

In addition, the closer we approach our own experience the less certain we can be about the status of our knowledge. It is not that immediate experience cannot be classed as 'knowledge', nor that the gaining of knowledge does not classify as 'experience'; it is that the epistemological character of either becomes less fixed. Whosoever steps over the line that conventionally separates the scholar from the critic - a line that is always being conventionally redrawn - must have unusual sensitivity to the terrain upon which he or she is standing; we are walking a treacherous ground on which the indicative can suddenly turn into the imperative, and where the general rules for the detection of special interest and humbug have been suspended.

Accordingly, I have decided to end this book in a critical rather than scholarly mode; so allowing the personal and the polemic, which have had a stealthy existence in the forgoing pages, to step out into the open.

* * * *

'Architecture in its infancy was colourful and richly decorated; it should gain colour and meaningful decoration again.' Gottfried Semper 1834

'Every strong tide of taste has its compensating ebb. To the doctrine of "richness" succeeded the doctrine of functionalism. In the third decade of the twentieth century we voluntarily renounced many of the pleasures of pattern. In the fourth decade these pleasures have been completely withheld from us. How will pattern begin again in Europe? Time alone can answer.' Joan Evans, 1950

Today the possibility of achieving a consistent modern decorative style, in the manner foreseen by nineteenth-century theorists, seems utterly unlikely and at first sight undesirable. In large areas of design we seem bound to a wheel of ever more ignorant revivalisms, or a patronising enthusiasm for 'ethnic' and other sources. We are truly in that condition that Wornum feared - the loss of 'distinct expression'.

But there is a duty intelligently to resist his cultural pessimism, since its fruits are the worship of power and inward emigration. In that resistance it is also essential not to run into the embrace of a commercial populism and see in the 'mixture of all elements' a kind of emancipation from the necessities of judgement. There is, indeed, an ethical issue buried in these multiplying possibilities. Between conflicting demands, what can legislate but a higher court? To use recent terminology - we must have our 'master narratives', or judgements of quality and priority become impossible.

Such narratives, as will be understood from the foregoing, have to be developed critically and not as systems of total explanation and prescription. What makes the project of the 'South Kensington school' objectionable today, in ideological terms, is its claim to universality. It is not that there may not be 'laws','universals' or 'constants' of decorative expression, but that to appropriate the notion to one's own practice is imperialistic. At the same time we cannot refuse some narrative, since even to deny the existence of ordering principles is itself a form of explanation.

Looking about us, we can identify general strategies at work through which contemporary decoration can be sustained and made meaningful.

These may appear to be competing narratives, but none, I think, amount to a 'discourse' in the sense I have been describing. Their theoretical description is likely to be within the terms of 'popular culture', and to be conceived synchronously, in relation to one another in simultaneity, rather than extended through time. However, it may be that fresh theoretical insights would reveal greater unity and continuity than at present seems graspable. This book, for reasons discussed above, does not attempt to provide a guide to the immediate scene; it can only comment upon it from the perspective of its own historical account.

The first general strategy is the persistence of the principle of assemblage, so ardently pursued by Lord Leighton. The ingenuity with which groups and individuals can mix and match extremely heterogeneous material and thereby create highly recognisable and consistent, though ephemeral, styles is a function of the disappearance of norms of taste, and the overwhelming abundance of goods which the past three decades have brought about. It is as if the essential principles of the Aesthetic Movement had become diffused through the entire population. It is not, however, a strategy dependent on this abundance, since the same features are exhibited worldwide, in less affluent and even poverty-stricken societies. The way in which 'ethnic' patterns and garments are taken over and adapted by the 'developed' world is mirrored by the reverse process. This mirror-image is not isomorphic, since the exchange is not by peoples of equal power ; but its consequences, in terms of styles and the interchanging and mixing of styles must be far-reaching.

The relations between this practice of assemblage and the possibilities offered by electric and electronic communications (and the availability of editing and recording techniques) is a matter for conjecture; but it does seem certain that the aesthetics of assemblage are a principal strategy at work today.

Another is the continuance of the critical tradition in the form of regional and localist movements. Regional and local styles developed out of economic and technical constraints; so when almost any other style would be as cheap or as costly, what are we doing when we adopt a localism? As viewed through this book, the critical tendency brings together in intellectual and practical coalition the popular resentment at the shock of continual modernisation with an educated defence of established and codified cultural identity. This is a permanent characteristic of every modern society. The oddity arises when this critical stance becomes itself the norm. It may be possible to see in this dilemma a process whereby cultural institutions are being redefined on local or regional bases as a counter to the transnational organisation of production. The hegemony has not lessened at all, it is just a little more difficult to see.

Allied to this is the cult of the old-fashioned. This manifests itself in many forms, and sometimes appears to be the main guiding force in English taste. At its cruder levels we observe it in the auction rooms; in its more fruitful aspect it can be seen in the present re-evaluation of Ruskin's writings. Now that we are freed from the simple-minded version of 'modernism', it is possible to look again at the critical tradition and to discover in it critiques of consumerism, unlimited production, and the cultural vandalism of capital's expansion which make much more sense to us than they did some decades previously. The development of a general 'ecological' awareness makes the arguments of the the Arts and Crafts Movement far more appealing than they were. That these movements of thought are also implicated in a resentment at national decline, and are full of compensatory sentimentality, does not invalidate their main premise.

The position taken by this book, however, is that popular resentment and an educated anti-Kantianism is wholly incapable of providing a sufficent base for a modern culture, though it does provide for sub-cultures and pockets of apparent 'alternative' diversity that everywhere inhabit world civilisation much like the birds that inhabit the crocodile's mouth. An ecological understanding (which would include a reasoned respect for old-fashioned methods) would seem to lead toward an extension of science and technology, and not its reverse. What this would mean for the decorative arts is of course very difficult to imagine, but if my assumption is right that decoration is in some sense a natural aspect of our species, then a renewed critical tradition has much to offer.

What appears to be essential here is a renovation along the lines proposed by Frampton in his 'critical regionalism'.[21] The aim of a critical regionalism would be to balance respect for locality with a refusal of easy neo-vernacular models, to maintain a creative tension between the global and the local.

Another strategy is a renovated and self-critical 'modernism'. (I am rather loathe to use that word, since the tenor of this study has been to question the notion of the unitary modernist movement, but for brevity's sake it must stand.) Such a position will treat historical 'modernism' as itself a source of critical positions, critical of the current material culture, its ideological assumptions and above all its prodigal waste. Once again, it is not at all clear how or in what form such a practice would produce 'decoration', though it has and does produce powerful architecture, but by being aware of the discourse it maintains the utopian possibility of a 'style-less' unconsumable style. Such a position is, in some important respects, ironic and retrospective; but it also seeks to recover social and intellectual optimism.

In this context it is interesting to remark on the persistence of floral and pictorial surface pattern, in chintzes and wallpapers; a survival which continues down to this present day the opposition between fact and fancy with which the discourse began. A survey of mail order catalogues reveals the same opposition between abstract flat pattern and deep-space pictorialism which so aggravated Mr Gradgrind. This opposition still bears with it the assumption of 'moderniser versus the modernised', and speaks of complex social distinctions.

It is also possible to be confident, following this study, about those presumptions and practices that will lead nowhere. The first of these is, clearly, an uncritical concept of 'tradition' or 'cultural identity'. Indeed, if we have thought at all about the discourse of decoration we shall see that it closes forever the door upon such notions as an unproblematic 'cultural tradition'. It is probably better to think of modern life as being, by nineteenth-century criteria, post-cultural. It seems certain that the unfolding of the immanent possibilities of social and artistic activity cannot now take place within the existing concept of 'a culture' taken as distinct from 'another culture'. The civil and technical organisation of human life depends now and forever upon global similarity and shared fate. Under such conditions, the re-ification of differences as 'cultures' and the pursuit of 'traditional' style must end in pastiche.

This is why an informed study of decoration is useful; it serves to sharpen that self-critical spirit without which local differences, traditions and identities simply come to serve as the stalking-horses of entirely different interests. Allied to this is the ever fainter spirit of 'post-modernism', the ghost in the calculator. The more one considers the discourse, the more one comes to recognise that 'post-modern' attitudes are a continuous feature of an ever-changing modernity. The concept as recently used is logically parasitic upon the prior assumption of a clearly defined and unitary 'modernism', which this study has consistently questioned.

The likelihood of a 'craft'-generated revival of decorative art seems also remote; the values and professional practices of the manual crafts have been continuously absorbed into those of the fine arts in recent decades.[22] More and more, imaginative craft-work has tended toward an 'autonomy' modelled on that of the fine arts.. While we can imagine a recovery of a craft-based decoration through 'critical regionalism', this would depend entirely on the prior architectural programme.

There are doubtless other possibilities through which meaningful decoration and enriching ornament can enter our lives, or be still further evacuated from them, but in the nature of things, they are hard to see; the present is not an object on which we can reflect. There is always a sense in which immediate experience is completely inexplicable. My hope is that what I have written will have provided a framework or general set of ideas which the reader may find useful, and through within which we can think constructively about the beauty and significance of our decoration.

Notes

1. White, H. *Tropics of Discourse* (1978) intro.
2. 'The relation between the words art and industry, fine arts and industrial art, industry and design, and the relations between these types of couplets constitute a special discourse on that paradise that capitalism would become if only one could reconcile the differences that they suppose. A paradise realised through the perfect harmonization of production and consumption.' Rifkin, A. 'Success Disavowed: the Schools of Design in mid-century Britain. (An Allegory)' in *The Journal of Design History* Vol.1. No.2. 1988 pp.89-102.
3. For detailed analysis of Committee membership and its intentions *see* Rhodes, J.G. 'Ornament and Ideology' unpublished PhD Thesis, Harvard University, 1984.
4. Owen Jones' long-standing interest in Egyptian and Islamic decoration should be seen in this context. His colleague Gottfried Semper wrote in an article of 1834 that 'Architecture in its infancy was colourful and richly decorated; it should gain colour and meaningful decoration again'. (See Mallgrave, 1983).
5. *See* Gombrich, E., (1979) p.12 & p.251.
6. *See* Brolin (1985)for discussions of this theme.
7. Bourdieu (1984) pp.41-42 and 56-57.
8. *See* Rhodes (1984) p.210.
9. ref. CRM, Hughes etc.10.
10. *See* Menocal (1981) for discussion.
11. *See* especially Jones (1856), which sets a pattern followed by numerous subsequent writers.
12. *See* the writings of Adrian Stokes and Anton Ehrenzweig, which employ psychoanalytic theory to analyse our response to surface texture, pattern and figure/ground relations. *See also* Gombrich (1979), ch.5, and his references to perceptual psychology.
13. All quotes from the 1987 edition published by Architectural Press, London . (James Dunnet trans.)
14. For details of Le Corbusier's education *see* Turner, *The Education of Le Corbusier*, (New York, 1977).
15. For an introduction to this difficult area, *see* Yates, *The Art of Memory* (London, 1966), pp.250-1, which deals with the 'imageless' teaching methods of the Protestant reformers and serves as a starting point for further investigation.
16. Le Corbusier,(1987), p.188.
17. *See* Collins (1965) p.265ff. (also Maschek, Banham etc,)
18. *See* Le Corbusier (1970), A. Ozenfant (1952) and the writings of Charles Henry, Humbert de Superville and others.
19. Piet Mondrian in *CIRCLE* (1937) p.52. and the essays and lectures of Theo van Doesburg.
20. For discussion *see* Tafuri (1976).
21. Frampton, K. (1985).
22. Fuller, P. (1983). *See also* the review of 'Textiles North' for a discussion of contemporary craft and 'the crisis of meaningful pattern and effective ornamentation.'

—Bibliography—

I have thought it useful to divide the bibliography into general and thematic sections. Under 'general' I include books and articles I have found useful at all points in my research; and under 'thematic' I have selected a number of salient themes which the reader may wish to pursue in more detail. Not all the texts given below are referred to directly, and some have little to do with decoration; much of the background study is assumed.

General

Berg, M. *The Age of Manufactures; Industry, Innovation and Work in Britain 1700-1820*, Fontana Press, London, 1985. A really useful survey of the general historical background.

Bourdicu, P. *Distinctions*, Routledge, Kegan Paul; London, 1984. Though this is a survey of contemporary French taste and social preferences, its methods and conclusions are highly relevant to this study.

Brett, D. 'Quantities and Qualities: arts and manufactures 1830-1930; a study of the philosophy and ideology of design reform.' Unpublished PhD thesis, Royal College of Art 1984.

Brett, D. 'The Interpretation of Ornament' in *Journal of Design History* Vol.1. No.2. 1988 pp.103 -112. The starting point of this book.

Brolin, B.C. *Flight of fancy; the banishment and return of ornament*, Academy Editions, London, 1985. A seriously wrong-headed book that is full of good material and acute observations.

Conrads, U. ed. *Programs and Manifestoes on 20th Century Architecture*, M.I.T. Press Cambs. Mass., 1970. Contains Loos' manifesto 'Ornament and Crime'.

Crook, J.M. *The Dilemma of Style; Architectural Ideas from the Picturesque to the Post-Modern*, London, 1986.

Davidoff, L. & Hall, C. *Family Fortunes; Men and Women of the English Middle Class 1780-1850*, Hutchinson, London, 1987. Important background reading to the development of home decoration.

Denvir, B. *The Late Victorians; Art, Design and Society 1852-1910*, Longman, London, 1988. An excellent compilation of contemporary documents, criticism etc.

Durant, S. *Ornament; a survey of decoration since 1830*, London, 1986. A survey of styles, done in great detail and with great learning.

Durant, S. *The Decorative Designs of C.F.A.Voysey*, The Lutterworth Press, Cambridge, 1990.

Eastlake, C. *Hints on Household Taste*, London, 1868 (Dover Publ. reprint New York 1969).

Evans, J. *Style in Ornament*, Oxford, 1950.

Forty, A. *Objects of Desire; Design and Society 1750-1980* Thames and Hudson, London 1986. An essential book!

Girouard, M. *Sweetness and Light; the Queen Anne movement 1860-1900*, Oxford, 1977.

Gloag, J. *Victorian Comfort; a Social History of Design from 1830-1900*, A. and C. Black, London, 1961.

Gombrich, E. *The Sense of Order*, Phaidon, London, 1979. A necessary book!

Gombrich, E. *Art and Illusion*, Phaidon, London, 1968.

Habermas, J. *Knowledge and Human Interests*, Heinemann, London, 2nd. ed. 1978

Halen, W. *Christopher Dresser*, Phaidon/Christie, London, 1990. The only biography of this remarkable man; excellent on design and business, less interested in ideas.

Haug, W. *Critique of Commodity Aesthetics; Appearance, Sexuality and Advertising in Capitalist Society*, Polity Press, Cambridge, 1986.

Heller, A. *A Theory of Feelings* van Gorcum, Assen (NL), 1979.

Heller, A. *Everyday Life*, Routledge, Kegan Paul, London, 1984.

Hobsbawn, E. & Ranger, T. eds. *The Invention of Tradition*, Cambridge U.P., 1980.

Jones, O. *The Grammar of Ornament*, Day and Sons, London, 1856.

Naylor, G. *The Arts and Crafts Movements*, Studio Vista, London, 1971.

Pevsner, N. *Some Architectural Writers of the Nineteenth Century*, Clarendon Press, Oxford, 1972.

Pevsner, N. *Studies in Art, Architecture and Design*, Thames and Hudson, London 1968.

Schmeichen, J.A. 'Reconsidering the Factory, Art Labour, and the Schools of Design in 19th Century Britain' in *Design Issues* Vol. 7 No.2. Spring 1990. pp.58-69. A useful recent article.

Wiener, M. *English Culture and the Decline of the Industrial Spirit 1850-1980*, Cambridge U.P., 1981.

Wornum, R. *Analysis of Ornament; the Characteristics of Styles etc.*, Chapman and Hall, London, 7th ed. 1882.

The 'South Kensington School'

Ashwin, C. *Art Education; Documents and Policies*, London, 1975.

Bell, Q. *The Schools of Design*, London, 1963.

Cole, Sir H. *Fifty Years of Public Work*, London, 1884.

Dyce, W. *The Drawing Book of the Government Schools of Design*, Chapman and Hall, London, 1843.

Frayling, C. *The Royal College of Art; One Hundred and Fifty years of Art and Design*, London, 1987.

Logan, F.M. *The Growth of Art in American Schools*, Harper, New York, 1955.

Macdonald, S. *The History and Philosophy of Art Education*, London, 1970.

Physick, J. *The Victoria and Albert Museum; the History of Its Building*, London, 1982.

Rhodes, J.G. 'Ornament and Ideology: a study in mid-19th century British Design Theory' unpublished PhD thesis, Harvard University, 1983.

Rifkin, A. 'Success Disavowed; the Schools of Design in mid-nineteenth century Britain, (An Allegory)', in *The Journal of Design History* Vol.1, No.2. 1988 pp.89-102.

Sutton, G. *Artisan or Artist; a history of the teaching of Arts and Crafts in English Schools*, Pergamon Press, London, 1967.

'Normative' Theory and Art Botany

Colquhoun, A. 'Typology and Design Method' (1969) reprinted in *Essays in Architectural Criticism*, ed. K. Frampton, M.I.T. Press, Cambridge, Mass., 1981.

Dresser, C. 'Botany as Adapted to the Arts and Art Manufacturing' in *The Art Journal* Vol.20 (1857) and Vol.21 (1858) A series of eleven articles of great interest.

Dresser, C. *The Art of Decorative Design*, London, 1862.

Dresser, C. 'Ornamentation considered as a high art' in *Journal of the Society of Arts* Vol.XIX, 1871 pp.217-26 and 352.

Dresser, C. *Principles of Decorative Design*, London 1873. For a complete list of Dresser's writings, see Halen (1990).

Durant, S. 'Aspects of the Work of C. Dresser' Unpublished MPhil thesis, Royal College of Art, 1973.

Ettlinger, L. 'On Science, Industry and Art; some theories of Gottfried Semper' in *Architectural Review* Vol.136 (1964).

Forbes, E. Article in *The Art Journal Illustrated Catalogue of the Great Exhibition*, London, 1851.

Jespersen, J.K. 'Owen Jones 'The Grammar of Ornament' of 1856; Field Theory in Victorian Design at the Mid Century.' Unpublished PhD thesis, Brown University, 1984.

Mallgrave, H.F. 'The Idea of Style; Gottfried Semper in London' Unpublished PhD thesis, University of Philadelphia, 1983.

Maschek, J. 'The Carpet Paradigm; critical prolegomena to a theory of flatness' in *Arts Magazine* Sept. 1976 pp.82-105.

Poe, E.A. 'The Philosophy of Furniture' in *Complete Works* Vol.XIV New York 1902; repr. 1965.

Redgrave, S.& R. *A Century of Painters*, London, 1886.

Redgrave, R. 'Passages from the Lectures on the Study of Botany by the Designer' in *Journal of Design and Manufactures* Vol.3. 1850 pp.97-100.

Steadman, P. *The Evolution of Designs; biological analogy in architecture and the applied arts*, Cambridge U.P., 1979.

'Critical' Theory

Collingwood, W.G. *The Philosophy of Ornament etc.*, Geo. Allen, Orpington, 1883.

Eastlake, C. *A History of the Gothic Revival*, London, 1872.

Ferriday, P. 'The Oxford Museum' in *Architectural Review* Dec. 1962. pp.408-416. The best published account of this building.

Garrigan, K.O. *Ruskin on Architecture; his thought and influence*, Univ. of Wisconsin, Madison. 1973.

Naylor, G. ed. *William Morris by Himself; designs and writings*, London, 1988. A magnificent book which serves as a good introduction to the huge literature on and by William Morris.

Ruskin, J. *The Elements of Drawing*, 3rd ed. Geo.Allen, Orpington, 1900.

Ruskin, J. *The Eagle's Nest*, London, 1872.

Ruskin, J. *Proserpina*, Geo. Allen, Orpington, 1872.

Ruskin, J. *The Two Paths; being lectures on art and its application to decoration and manufactures, delivered in 1858-9*, Geo. Allen, Orpington, 1884 ed..

The literature by and on Ruskin is vast; these are the books I have consulted most often.

Sheehy, J. *The Rediscovery of Ireland's Past; the Celtic Revival 1830-1930*, Thames and Hudson, London, 1980.

Watkin, D. *The English Vision; the picturesque in architecture, landscape and garden design*, Murray, London, 1982.

Colour in Architecture and Orientalism

Darby, M. 'Owen Jones and the eastern Ideal' unpublished PhD thesis. Univ. of Reading, 1974. The only lengthy treatment of Jones.

Darby, M. *The Islamic Perspective*, exh. catalogue. World of Islam Festival Trust. London, 1983. A very useful source.

Darby, M. & van Zanten, D. 'Owen Jones Iron Buildings of the 1850's' in *Architectura* VI 1974 pp.53-73.

Middleton, R. *The Beaux Arts and 19th Century French Architecture*, M.I.T. Press, Cambridge, Mass., 1982.

Nochlin L. 'The Imaginary Orient' in *Art in America*, May, 1983.

Said, E. *Orientalism*, Routledge Kegan Paul, London, 1978.

Sweetman, J. *The Oriental Obsession; Islamic inspiration in British and American Art and Architecture 1500-1920*, Royal Academy catalogue. London, 1984.

Tawadros, C. 'Foreign Bodies: art history and the discourse of 19th century orientalist art.' in *Third Text* 3/4 Spring and Summer 1988 pp.51-68.

van Zanten, D. *The Architectural Polychromy of the 1830's*, London, 1977.

De Stijl etc.

Beckett, J. 'The Abstract Interior' in *Towards a New Art*, Tate Gallery Catalogue, London, 1980.

Hill, A. ed. *D.A.T.A.; Directions in Art, Theory and Aesthetics*, Faber and Faber; London, 1968.

Stead, P. Quotations in Sample 26 are from the records of Peter Stead, to whose assistance and inspiration I am indebted. Notes on the collaboration can be found in *Aujourd'hui* Sept 1955 and in *Architectural Design* July 1959 and *The Architecture of Technology* ed. T. Crosby. London 1961.

Wilson, C. St.J. 'Gerrit Rietveld 1888-1964' in *Architectural Review* Vol.136 (1964) PP.3999-402.

American Connections

Menocal, N.G. *Architecture as Nature; the transcendentalist idea of Louis Sullivan*, Univ. of Wisconsin, Madison, 1981.

O'Gorman, J.F. *The Architecture of Frank Furness*, Philadelphia Mus. of Art/ Philadelphia, 1973.

Ross, D.W. *A Theory of Pure Design*, Boston and New York, 1907

Ross, D.W. *On Drawing and Painting*, Boston and New York, 1912

Stein, R.B. *John Ruskin and Aesthetic Thought in America 1840-1900*, Harvard U.P., Cambridge, Mass., 1967.

Sullivan, L.H. *A System of Architectural Ornament; according with a philosophy of man's powers*, Eakins Press, New York, repr. 1967.

Connections in Continental Europe

Englemann, P. *Ludwig Wittgenstein; a memoir*, Blackwell, Oxford 1967. Englemann was a pupil of Loos and he helped the philosopher in the design of the house.

Gravagnuolo, B. *Adolf Loos; Theory and Works*, New York 1982. Much the best intro. to Loos available; it sets 'Ornament and Crime' into its context very clearly.

Indiana, G. 'Ludwig Wittgenstein, Architect' in *Art in America* Jan. 1985. pp.112-133. A learned and passionate article.

Janik, A. & Toulmin, S. *Wittgenstein's Vienna*, New York, 1973.

Leitner, B. *The architecture of Ludwig Wittgenstein; a documentation*, N.Y. Univ. Press, New York 1966; see also *Art Forum* Feb. 1970 and *Architectural Design* June, 1971.

Muthesius, H. *The English House*, TTR. J. Seligman, London, 1979 (first ed. Berlin, 1904).

Newman, J.O. & Smith, J.H. eds. *Adolf Loos; Spoken into the Void. Collected Essays 1897-1900*, M.I.T.Press, Cambridge, Mass., 1982. A collection of essays and articles, all interesting and some important.

Schorske, C.E. *Fin de Siecle Vienna; Politics and Culture*, New York, 1981.

Silverman, D. *Art Nouveau in Fin-de-Siecle France*, Univ. of California Press, 1989.

Volkov, S. *The Rise of Popular Anti-Modernism in Germany; the urban master artisans 1873-1896*, Princeton U.P. 1978.

Printed Textile and Wallpapers

Chapman, S.D. *The Cotton Industry in the Industrial Revolution*, Macmillan, London, 1972.

Entwhistle, E.A. *Wallpapers of the Victorian Era*, Lewis, Leigh on Sea, 1964.

Greysmith, D. 'The Impact of Technology on Printed Textiles in the Early Nineteenth Century' in *Design and Industry; the effects of industrialisation and technical change on design*, ed. Hamilton N. The Design Council, London, 1980.

Oman, C.C. & Hamilton, J. *Wallpapers: a history and illustrated catalogue of the collection of the Victoria and Albert Museum*, London, 1982. An indispensable book.

Turnbull, G. *A History of the Calico Printing industry in Great Britain*, J. Sherrat. Altrincham, 1951.

Positivism etc.

Comte, A. *The Positive Philosophy of Auguste Comte*, tr. H. Martineau (1855) reprint AMS Press, New York, 1974.

Manual, F.E. *The New World of Henri Saint-Simon*, Univ. of Notre Dame Press, 1963.

Simon, W.M. *European Positivism in the 19th century; an essay in intellectual history*, Kennikat Press, New York, 1972.

Wright, T.R. *The Religion of Humanity; the impact of Comtean Positivism on Victorian Britain*, Cambridge U.P., 1986.

Some Books from the Introduction and the Postscript

Collins, P. *Changing Ideals in Modern Architecture*, London, 1965.

Foster, H. ed. *Post Modern Culture*, Pluto Press, London, 1985.

Frampton, K. 'Toward a Critical Regionalism' in Foster ed. (1985).

Fuller, P. *The Naked Artist; art and biology*, London, 1983.

Habermas, J. 'Modernity - an incomplete project' in Foster ed. (1985).

Le Corbusier, *The Decorative Art of Today*, The Architectural Press, London, 1987.

Tafuri, M. *Architecture and Utopia*, MIT Press, Cambridge, Mass., 1976.

White, H. *Tropics of Discourse*, London, 1978.

— Index —

Index of Names

Concepts, Movements and Institutions